EFFECTIVE
SELLING AND
SALES MANAGEMENT

EFFECTIVE SELLING AND SALES MANAGEMENT

How to Sell Successfully and Create a Top Sales Organization

Gini Graham Scott, Ph. D.

ASJA Press
New York   Lincoln   Shanghai

Effective Selling and Sales Management
How to Sell Successfully and Create a Top Sales Organization

ASJA Press
an imprint of iUniverse, Inc.

iUniverse books may be ordered through booksellers or by contacting:

iUniverse
2021 Pine Lake Road, Suite 100
Lincoln, NE 68512
www.iuniverse.com
1-800-Authors (1-800-288-4677)

Because of the dynamic nature of the Internet, any Web addresses
or links contained in this book may have changed
since publication and may no longer be valid.

The views expressed in this work are solely those of the author and
do not necessarily reflect the views of the publisher, and the publisher hereby
disclaims any responsibility for them.

Originally published by Brick House Publishing

ISBN: 978-0-595-46486-9

Printed in the United States of America

Contents

EFFECTIVE
SELLING AND
SALES MANAGEMENT

Introduction

This book is written to help the many people today, from entrepreneurs and small business people to managers of corporate sales groups, who have products or services to sell. Whether you have your own business or are part of a larger organization, whether you want to begin by selling yourself, work with a handful of sales people, or are building a large sales group, this book is designed to help you do it.

Today, as never before, sales and marketing are the keys to success in any business enterprise. The marketplace has become so competitive, with many new products and services jostling for attention, that good sales people and good sales techniques are more important than ever in gaining an edge.

The signs are everywhere. Large advertising agencies are getting even larger. Licensing has become a major source of income in industries that produce books, films, dolls, and toys, where big bucks buy big, splashy promotions for popular commercial characters. And sales people, like John Scully of Apple Computers, are gaining more and more visibility and receiving higher and higher salaries, more than a million dollars annually in some cases, because they are considered so important to the success of a company.

What does this mean for the owner or manager of a small business? For a new sales manager in an established company?

For the entrepreneur, it means that you've got to sell well yourself, or get someone good to do it if you can't. And if you want your business to grow and expand successfully, you've got to recruit good sales people and develop an effective sales organization, or hire someone who can.

For the new sales manager, it means that selling is now what you must teach and direct, not simply do well yourself. And it means that effective recruitment, development and management of a sales group is how you will be measured for success.

Unfortunately, many entrepreneurs and many managers of established businesses don't know how to create or mobilize a good sales effort. For example, when Andrea T., an experienced chef, tried to launch a small catering service, she tried to do most of the promoting and selling herself. But she disliked it, wasn't particularly good at sales, and preferred to spend her time creating hors d'oeuvres. She would have done better to recruit one or more sales people to sell her services.

Tom G. had a different problem. He liked sales and was very aggressive. But when he became sales manager in a medium-sized specialty gifts company, he found it hard to coordinate and motivate his sales people. He knew what to do himself, but he didn't know how to convey that knowledge, or how to motivate others through training and support. As a result, the company perpetually suffered sales volume lower than expected, and a high turnover of sales people who quit out of frustration.

George L., on the other hand, had the basic skills of managing people and the enthusiasm to build a successful distribution organization, selling a new specialty foods product through direct sales. But he didn't know how to develop an effective sales organization. So his good ideas, management skills, and enthusiasm languished.

The information and advice in this book are based on my own experience in organizing sales groups in the field of health, food, consumer savings, and travel, and in consulting about selling and marketing with the owners and sales managers of dozens of companies. From this experience and additional informal interviews with hundreds of other business people I found that:

Many creative or technical people running their own companies don't know how to sell their own products or services, and they don't know how to get others to do it.

Many people who have good sales skills themselves, don't know to teach others to do what they do. Their sales people are ineffective.

Some people manage the initial stages of building a sales group well, but then have trouble coordinating activities and maintaining group enthusiasm and commitment.

Some new business people are unfamiliar with already organized networks of sales representatives and distributors in their own fields, and fail to take advantage of these sales channels for their own products or services.

Many companies lack good sales or training materials, or don't effectively adapt materials they do have to meet the needs of their sales people.

This book is designed to provide solutions to all of these problems and to help you build sales or a sales team successfully. Like a road map, it can help you chart your course, but then it's up to you to carry out your plans to reach your destination or goal.

1
Creating Sales Materials

When most people decide to buy something, they already have an idea of what they want, an idea created by advertising and publicity they have already seen. Today, all customers expect this, be they consumers, retailers, or wholesalers. They want to see something that briefly positions and presents the product, such as a brochure, flyer, or catalog sheet. And in the case of some products, they even expect to see films, slide presentations, and videotapes.

What you have in the way of literature for your product or service really makes a difference, even if you are selling the same thing as someone else. People look on the quality of your literature as representative of your company.

A PERSONAL EXAMPLE

I have reacted the same way myself in making a buying decision. For instance, I attended a recent trade show looking for telephones to use in my new office. Several companies displayed telephones, all offered at about half the retail price since this was a trade show for company buyers only. One firm had a slick and glossy color brochure illustrating their phones; other firms had the same phones, but only black and white photo copies of product illustrations, and a price list.

I discovered that the phones I wanted were carried by all three wholesalers, though the one with the glossy color brochure was charging about two dollars a phone more than the others. Nevertheless I decided to get my phones from them. Why? Because their attractive catalog sheet made me feel more confident in their ability to deliver what I wanted. The high-quality catalog sheet made them seem solid and substantial as a company.

PURPOSES OF PROMOTIONAL MATERIALS

The particular promotional materials you need depend, of course, on the type of products and services you offer, how many you have, how complex they are to explain, and the like. The more complete your arsenal of materials, the better off you will be.

If you are in the early stages of a program, you can develop your materials as you go. In that case, it helps to get feedback from your customers on what they need. Promotional materials can be used to serve a number of purposes.

Attracting Attention

For example, fliers or brochures can be posted or left at meetings or included in a mailing to get a customer to call for information or place an order.

Presenting Product Benefits to a Customer

For example, a sales person can take some time at a presentation to review the material and use a brochure, information sheet, or presentation book to explain benefits and features, and gain credibility.

Giving the Prospect Something to Review

For example, if the customer isn't ready to make a purchase on the spot, a promotional brochure and order form may be what the customer needs as a reminder after your presentation, in order to think about the product, discuss it with others, or be reassured that it is really needed.

TYPES OF PROMOTIONAL MATERIALS

A typical collection of promotional materials includes, roughly in order of importance, the following items.

Presentation Book

If you're marketing an expensive product or service, or a variety of different products, a presentation book or manual can be an excellent tool for impressing your customer. It's a way systematically to present your various promotional materials by combining them together in an attractive book.

I like to put these materials together in a way that allows me easily to move them around to suit a particular presentation. A looseleaf book is good for this purpose, and I personally like clear-view binders, since you can slip in and out different title pages for the cover.

But leather and vinyl covers are good too and are especially well suited to expensive or customized products.

To be able to move materials around easily, I suggest using clear plastic sleeves with three holes. You can easily rearrange your materials, and add or drop items at will by simply putting them in or pulling them out of a sleeve.

Organization. Once you decide on the general order of your presentation, you can organize your supporting materials. It is important that the manual include what you want to cover, and that it be in a suitable sequence. Keep it clear and to the point. Pare out extraneous details.

In advertising, each frame of an ad is used to create a strong, powerful, well-directed message. Your sales manual should be structured that way.

For easy organization, separate each major section, such as Introduction, Product or Service, The Company, Close, with a divider or introduce it with a title page. You can use rub-on letters to make headlines on this page. Either rub them directly on to the divider or title page, or make a master copy of your title page layout on white paper. Then run off a copy on colored paper or good bond paper.

For technical product and marketing information, include an appendix. You won't discuss this in your initial presentation, but you have it if anyone asks. Finally, prepare a table of contents for easy reference.

Features. Useful additions to your manual include charts, graphs, photographs, and other visual materials. You may be able to get these from the company you represent or from support companies in the same field. For instance, in the travel field, brochures are available from companies, airlines and country tourist offices.

You can also put visual materials together fairly easily. Cut pictures out of a magazine to illustrate a point. Or transform sales figures into a bar graph to show that other customers are buying your product or service in increasing numbers.

Local touches can help, too. For example, if you have organized/or participated in a local promotion, such as a trade show or product demonstration, or have pictures of people in your company at work, use this to create a more personal style.

Brochure or Catalog Sheet

Some people just getting started use only fliers or order forms. But with some notable exceptions (such as an impulse product that immediately sells itself or a person offering services who already has an established name), a brochure or catalog sheet is crucial. Your brochure describes you, your company, and its services or products; a catalog sheet or full catalog features your products. When these materials are good, they represent you and what your products or services stand for. They're calling cards for you and your company.

Make your promotional materials as good as you can. Put a lot of thought into what you want to say and how you want to say it. Take into consideration your primary target market and design your brochure or catalog to appeal to this group. Are you selling to the ultimate customer? If so, ask yourself, who is most likely to buy? Women or men? Urban sophisticates? Suburban couples? Older people? Middle aged? Young adults?

In designing your material, look at what other people marketing to a similar audience are already doing. That will give you an idea of the kind of look or style to use. If you are selling to a wholesaler or retailer, design your brochure or catalog sheet accordingly so that the materials are even more appealing than usual.

I also recommend using a professional graphics designer. If you've got a really good design sense, you can get away with going directly to a printer and choosing the typeface and paper stock and making the layout yourself. But if you're uncertain about this or if this is your first brochure, I suggest hiring a professional. Professionals know what they are doing, and will save you time and money in the long run. Your brochure or catalog sheet is such an important selling tool, it pays to do it right.

Price List and Order or Sign-Up/Application Form

Some people include order forms in their brochures or catalogs. That's fine if you know what your prices are going to be for the life of these materials or if you expect to produce an updated brochure or catalog in time for the next price change.

However, it makes more sense to have a separate price list and order or sign-up/application form, which can be easily printed on an as-needed basis. Then you can more easily and inexpensively change your prices or terms; you don't have to redo the catalog or brochure itself.

Also give some thought to the format of your order form, since a well-designed format can help increase orders and serve as a research tool to gather information about your customers to better target your market. (Order forms are such important selling tools that there are even seminars and workshops devoted to them alone.) Briefly, be sure your order form has these elements:

Name, address, and zip code.

Credit-card check-off boxes with spaces for card number, expiration date, and phone number (assuming that you accept credit cards).

A list of products with their prices and space to check off the quantities desired, followed by spaces to write in the total price if there is room. Or leave space so the buyer can write in product names. This makes it easy for customers to order.

Spaces where a person can easily add up subtotals and add tax (if applicable) plus freight and handling.

A few brief questions for fill-in or check-off, if you want information about your customers. For instance, one woman for whom I consulted had a small catalog with products for cat lovers, and she asked such questions in it as, "Do you have a cat?" and "About how much do you spend on products with pictures of cats on them each year?"

Questions about credit worthiness (such as references about previous purchases or a bank name), if you need credit information for a COD or pay-after-delivery order.

Similarly, sign-up or registration forms or applications can be both sales and information tools. These materials are usually more appropriate when you're selling a program or service, rather than a product, or when a customized and expensive product is involved. In this case, you can get fairly detailed in what you ask customers.

Flyers

Flyers are ideal for drawing attention to your product or service and highlighting their benefits. They're a good introduction, and it is often more economical to use a flyer first and save your catalog sheets or brochures for more serious prospects.

Usually you can't use them for making the final sale. Buyers will want more information and reassurance about the qualities and advantages of the product or service than is offered in a flyer.

Among other purposes, I have used flyers to promote a customized service, describe a money-making opportunity, invite people to a product demonstration, highlight benefits, and offer more information on a product.

Graphics. You can make your own flyers fairly inexpensively, for less than $25. Graphic aides anyone can use are widely available. For example, use rub-on letters and a burnisher, available in art stores, to create good-looking headlines. To liven up your layout, use a rubber-stamp catalog or book of clip art for illustrations.

Rule lines for headlines with a light blue pencil and a ruler, then use scissors to cut up the headlines, artwork, and any typed copy. Use spray glue to paste them on a sheet of white paper. Use white artist's tape or correction fluid to clean up your final layout, and you're ready to make copies, preferably on colored paper. You can find all types in a paper supply store.

Copy. Keep it simple. Prepare flyer information as if you were writing an ad. Focus on a few key points, and use a larger size or special type of letter to highlight major ideas. Leave plenty of blank space around your copy so it is easy to read. Break copy into a few brief paragraphs to make it readable. Ask for action, such as inviting people to come to a particular event, call for more details, or ask for a product presentation in their homes.

Advertising Offprints

Copies of your advertising are ideal to show a customer that you're providing advertising support for your product or service. Today, given the plethora of advertising everywhere, customers often view advertising as reassurance that the product or service is good. Even if they haven't seen your ad, showing them your advertisements in a product presentation can add to your credibility.

You can use ads in a number of ways. Use the original, or a copy, in a presentation book to show to the customer. Turn a good strong visual ad into a flyer, and distribute or post it just like a flyer. Combine a copy of the ad with a letter and use it in an introductory mailing.

Use an ad agency to place ads if you have the budget to do so. If you do a substantial amount of advertising, the agency will take its 15% commission from the publication's regular charge for advertising space and you won't have to pay anything for this service. If you're doing only a small amount of advertising, it still may be worth paying a small fee for copy work and art. A good ad will more than pay for itself in the long run in better sales. Also, it will contribute to your image by attracting good sales people to your company.

Coupon Offers

Coupon offers are ideal for supplementing your brochure, price list, sign-up sheet or flyers. They give a bonus for acting now or before a certain date, or offer a better price if a person buys a certain package of services or products. They encourage a person to act.

As with flyers, you can create your own coupon offers by simply typing up the offer and embellishing the coupon with attractive graphics and headline type. Then print multiple copies on a page and cut them up.

Posters

Posters are good for certain kinds of products or services, especially where there is potentially broad appeal and you can dramatically highlight a special event or product benefit. Make sure your poster is consistent in appearance with the product or service you're advertising.

If you're not artistically talented, work with a local printer or artist. Or if you're just making a few posters with a limited amount of copy, hire some student artists at about $5 to $6 per hour. They should be able to create one or two posters an hour.

You will find that certain stores are receptive to putting up posters. Local bulletin boards may be good. Pick out locales that are likely to attract the type of person likely to use your product or service. For instance, if you've got a sports-related service, a sports shop would be ideal; for travel, perhaps try a camera shop or luggage store.

Besides making your own posters you can use special postering services when available. These services go around regularly with posters and flyers and put them up in major stores and on bulletin boards that allow them.

In-Store Display Coupons

Coupons displayed in stores are designed to appeal to ultimate customers. You can use them if you have a system to give store owners credit for leads they refer, or for orders generated directly from the coupons they hand out.

Promotional Letters

These letters are good if used in conjunction with a prior phone call to establish interest. The letter is designed to accompany sales material directed to the customer and to open the door for further contact, such as a follow-up phone call to get the order or to set up an appointment for a product or service presentation.

Sheet of Common Questions and Answers

In marketing some products and services, you'll find that some questions repeatedly come up, even if you have a brochure that covers them. People don't always remember everything they read, or they may want clarification.

Then, too, there are certain topics you can't always cover in a brochure but can cover in a more detailed explanation sheet. Here you can tell how your product differs or is better than a competing product or service, or the kind of special arrangements that are available.

To make up such a sheet, keep track of questions people ask and have your other sales people do the same. Then, take the questions that recur and write answers to them.

Publicity Materials

Once your product or service starts getting publicity, collect and use it to impress customers with whatever you're offering. For example, paste up published articles or photos and make copies of them to send out with promotional letters and put in your presentation book.

When you do a paste-up of such materials, make them look good. Include the full name of the publication in which they appeared and the date. Ideally, clip that information out of the publication, rather than typing it in. It will look more official that way.

When you have only a few clippings, putting them on a single page is fine. As they accumulate, you can make a collage of articles to show that your company is an expanding success.

Miscellaneous Articles and Information About Your Product

Even if you or your company receive no publicity you can use general articles published about your field. The closer the article comes to mentioning your type of product or service, the better. For example, if you're marketing a tax and financial planning service, create a handout with articles on how people are saving money through financial planning. If you're selling computers or computer consulting services, an article on the latest in computers might help.

Special Letters and Testimonials

If you receive letters of praise or testimonial statements, include them in your presentation to customers. These letters will impress your customers, especially in establishing credibility and broad support for whatever you're selling.

To get such letters and testimonials, simply write to the right people and tell them what you want. For example, when putting on one promotional event, I wrote to the mayor describing what we were doing and asked for a special letter or proclamation we could read at the event.

When I wanted support for a book I had published I called some people who had read it and asked if I could have a statement from them to use in my publicity. All of them agreed, and some even suggested that I write it myself and read it to them. It was an ideal way to get someone to say exactly what I wanted in order to promote my product. You can do the same.

Audio Tapes

Audio tapes on cassette are useful to give customers a more direct experience of testimonials or to impress them with the words of an expert. However, taped material should be short, no more than about 15 minutes, since most people's attention spans for such material are short.

To get testimonials, you can do a series of mini-interviews. You can even use the phone with the appropriate recording device. Ask a half dozen satisfied users of your product or service to say what they liked about it.

Be sure they give you written permission to use their comments as sales material. To get comments from an expert, you can take (with permission) comments from a talk by this person and string them together with the views of other experts to prove your point.

Slide Shows and Videos

Increasingly, slide shows and videos are being used in sales presentations. They're ideal to give customers a hands-on view of how your product or service is used, allowing them to imagine themselves in a customer or client role. Slide shows and videos can also help to explain and visually reinforce key points you make. If you are working with a large company or franchisor they may supply such aids. Or you can organize your own.

Even if your own efforts are not as slick and professional, it may not matter if you can sell with a personal touch. For example, in a travel sales group I once worked with, several of us put together our own slide shows from slides we had taken on trips. Also, we obtained a video presentation from a client who filmed his trip.

His film had a number of flaws, such as being weak in cutting, dialogue, editing and the like. But that didn't matter. What was most important to prospects was that they could identify with this person and his point of view; they could see themselves in his shoes going on a similar trip.

The films we got from tourist offices that we worked with were much better quality than our client's film, but we still used his at times because it had a nice personal touch. It showed that someone who actually went on one of our trips had come back an enthusiast.

With today's technology, it is easy to use and make copies of videos. I recommend using this format where you can. Slides and films can be transferred onto video tape for about 75 cents a minute. Then, once you have a video master tape, it costs about $20 to copy it commercially; or if you can hook up two VCRs yourself, the only cost is for blank video tape, about $6-$10 a reel.

DECIDING WHAT YOU NEED

Use the accompanying checklist to keep track of the promotional materials you choose, whether from those discussed above or others you learn about or develop from your experience. Review this checklist from time to time and modify it to suit your current situation.

Checklist of Promotional Materials

Item	Need	Already Have	Plan to Get Now	Later
Presentation Book				
Brochure				
Catalog Sheet				
Price List				
Order Form				
Sign-Up Form				
Flyers (fill in subject matter)				
Advertising Copies (identify)				
Coupon Offers				
Posters				
In-Store Display coupons				
Promotional Letters				
Common Questions and Answers				
Publicity Materials				
Articles and Product Information				
Letters and Testimonials				
Tapes				
Slide Shows				
Videos				

2
Getting Started

When you are first getting started running your own business, learning how to sell your products or services yourself is a good idea, for several reasons. First, it will give you an insight into how people respond to your product or service, so you can learn what works and how to adapt your program to take advantage of the responses.

Second, it will help you discover which sales techniques are the most effective, and you can pass this information on to your sales people later.

Third, you will develop a track record in selling your product or service which you can use to motivate your sales people. If you can get initial sales going, you can show there is a market, and that will help to get other sales people to share your enthusiasm.

Finally, your experience in selling will give you the confidence and assurance needed to lead and coordinate a sales group. Also, it will give you more authority, because you have done the selling yourself.

TEST THE MARKET FIRST

If you have a new product or service, you need to do some advance work, apart from preparing your sales literature, before you are ready sell. By doing a market survey, you'll have a better idea if your product is a good one, and therefore will be in a better position to sell it confidently yourself, or make the necessary changes in order to give yourself confidence.

In short, don't assume your product or service is great just because you and a few friends like it. Check it out in the marketplace before you get all geared up to sell it, to lessen the chance of finding that you have made a costly mistake.

Checking the Retail Market

If you will be selling to retailers, show a sample of your product to a few local stores. With small stores, you can often just drop in. With department stores, call and make an appointment to see the buyer.

See how buyers react. Are they interested in buying your product as is, or do they have suggestions for changes? Do they have any problems with the price? If so, maybe you can make some modification in the product to reduce the price. Do they have reservations about the packaging? If so, how can you improve it?

Are there problems with instructional materials accompanying the product? If so, how can they be modified? Would buyers prefer to see the product in a different color or style? What do they recommend?

Checking with Wholesalers and Sales Representatives

Another way to do some advance checking is to go to a trade show where sales representatives, manufacturers, and wholesalers are selling their products. Take your product around to reps or wholesalers who are selling similar products to find out if they would like to represent you. Most of them will be willing to give you a quick reading.

A caution: approach them at a time when show traffic is slow. Their first priority is to sell, not look at new products. Arrive early or stay late, because these times are usually slowest, or find a lull during the day.

When you show your product, be ready to identify a price point and describe how your product will be packaged. Then ask the same kinds of questions you would ask a retail buyer. Do they think the retail customer will like it? How do they feel about the price? Packaging? Color? Style?

EASY WAYS TO GET STARTED IN SELLING

Sell to Friends

Invite a few friends, business associates, or neighbors to a presentation at your home or office. People in small business do this all of the time. For example, women who run small customized dress businesses out of their homes regularly put on sales presentations for women they meet at business networking groups.

Sell to Groups

Tell the group leader or program chairman of an organization you belong to about your product or service and offer to put on a free event for them. They might be interested in a lecture on a topic related to your business, for example, on image if you're marketing beauty products or clothes, or on exercise techniques if you're selling a sports product.

Carry Your Literature

Carry packets of promotional literature with you. These might include an introductory flyer or brochure, a list of presentations you are giving and their locations, or a small sample of your product. Hand out these packets to the people you meet, suggesting they might like to try the product or use your service.

Put Up Posters and Leave Flyers

Put up posters or flyers at places you visit, such as campus buildings and bulletin boards, churches and community centers, supermarkets, coin-op laundries, and stores or restaurants that display posters and flyers.

Leave flyers for display at parties, meetings and conferences, and at your school or office. If you can, make an announcement about your product or service at such events, and then pass out flyers.

Your announcement will focus attention on your message and give you more credibility. It suggests you have the support of the organization holding the event.

Talk About What You Offer

Talk about your product or service, when appropriate, wherever you are. You can promote your product or business whatever you are doing. Just bring it up casually in the conversation when you talk to friends and business associates.

Emphasize the benefits of the product as appropriate. For example, if someone mentions having trouble losing weight and you are promoting a health product, use the opportunity to comment that you have something that can help, and then describe your product.

KNOW YOUR CUSTOMER

You need to be aware of two important aspects of the selling process, and keep them in mind as you work.

1. Before you sell your product or service, you are selling yourself, so you need to establish a comfortable rapport with your prospect so that person wants to buy from you.

2. You are selling to an individual, who has individual needs, wants, and desires. You want to tailor your message and presentation to that person.

Create Rapport

In retail selling in a store, people are used to getting right to the point. The customer is there for the express purpose of buying or at least considering the possibility of buying something. In many other sales situations, the seller must first take the time to make the prospect feel at ease and receptive, before beginning the sales process.

Make small talk. A common way to establish rapport is to start off an encounter with some small talk. If you are not already good at small talk, learn how to deliver a few lines of warm-up conversation easily so that you can break the ice wherever you are.

A good place to practice is in non-sales situations, such as a party, so that you can experiment with different approaches and discover what works for you, without risking loss of a sale.

The style you want to achieve is informal and light, yet sincere and heartfelt. In other words, you don't want to have small talk that sounds canned, leading your prospect to think, "Uh, oh, going to try to sell me something," or "Is this person for real?" Rather, you want to set the prospect at ease in a way that shows you care.

Observe cues. Pay attention to cues that tell how the prospect is reacting to you. If the body language is open, arms down, a smile, you can go on. But if the person seems rigid, appears tense, looks skeptical, you are receiving signals to hold off. Should you try to press on with your message when a prospect is not ready to hear you, and if he or she cannot appropriately move away, the prospect will tune you out.

Note Personality Types

People have different personality types that influence how they will respond to you and the way you present your message. A simple way to see this is to imagine you are on the telephone.

If you are talking with someone with a slow southern drawl, but you talk (and keep talking) rapid-fire, you will very soon lose the person. You need to slow yourself down to establish rapport.

Likewise, if you normally have a soft or gentle way of speaking and you connect with a high-powered type, you had better push you own presentation up to speed, or while you are trying to explain the call, the person will be thinking, "Ho hum."

Although there are a number of systems used to characterize personalities, I prefer to combine them into four types.

The **take-charge person** has a strongly developed ability to take in spoken information quickly. A leader: assertive, aggressive, direct, organized, interested in broad overviews and trends. Prefers others to be direct, to the point, to get behind and support his or her ideas and plans.

The **analyzer/explorer** has a well-developed visual sense, and likes seeing details presented logically. Cool, calm, detached, independent, curious. Likes to know how things fit together. Prefers others to be clear, organized, and offer a full picture. Likes others with analytical minds.

The **people person** experiences sensations and responds emotionally and expressively. Sensitive, dependent on others, concerned with details. Aware of and responsive to people. Wants things to go smoothly. Often a follower or helper. Prefers that others provide the details. Likes others who are warm and responsive.

The **conscientious planner** looks ahead and likes to feel certain about how things will be. Perceptive, quick to know. Organized, often critical, judgmental, opinionated, righteous. Has a good sense of what will happen and how things will turn out. Prefers that others be agreeable, receptive to his or her ideas. Likes others to be organized, self-assured and confident.

A person may be a mixture of types, but you will find that one personality style predominates. The descriptions above will help you figure out how to classify the people you meet and how best to interact with them.

ADAPT YOUR STYLE TO THE CUSTOMER

Adapt your style to what feels comfortable with that person and in the presentation. Some people are relaxed, casual, and friendly, while others feel more comfortable when you keep your distance.

If you're trying to sell something to a friend, you can be informal. But if you're with someone you don't know, being professional and formal is usually best, unless you get a clear message that they like informality.

Similarly, in selling to someone in a business, make your presentation organized and slick. When you talk to a housewife or factory worker, present your case in a more down-to-earth, personalized way.

In adapting your presentation to your prospect, take into account the following factors:

Your relationship to this person (friend, business associate, stranger).
Your prospect's occupational background, educational level, and main
    interests.
Your prospect's personal style (relaxed, casual, informal, warm and
    friendly versus distant, reserved, aloof, and formal).

You'll find you often make adjustments to others intuitively whether you pay attention to adapting or not. However, if you are aware of these factors and concentrate on really knowing about the other person, you can better fine tune the adjustments you make.

TAILOR YOUR APPROACH TO YOUR TARGET MARKET

Since everyone you contact has different wants and needs, and certain groups or types of individuals have special interests, think about how you can slant your approach to appeal to different markets. In this way you can emphasize the features of your program that are most likely to be of special interest to the particular individual or group you are contacting.

Although most sales people tend to vary their approach on an ad hoc basis as they contact people, it helps to think in advance about what you intend. Then you can be more systematic and efficient in using your advertising, flyers, promotional letters, and other materials.

To help you systematically adapt your marketing approach to your target audience, you can use the Target Market/Product Benefits Form to select the features or benefits that are most likely to interest each group.

List the key features or benefits of your product or service in column 1. List the types of individuals or groups you think might be most interested across the top of the form. In each column place a X to indicate special interest in a product feature or benefit. Indicate how important you think each feature or benefit might be to members of a group by rating it from 1, least important, to 5, most important.

Tailor your advertising, flyers, letters, and other promotional efforts to emphasize the features and benefits with special appeal to each group.

Target Market/Product Benefits Form

Product Features or Benefits	Types of Individuals or Groups Interested		
	1	2	3
1			
2			
3			
4			
5			
6			
7			

3
Selling Techniques

QUALIFYING: WHAT THE CUSTOMER WANTS

To make selling work, you must direct your message to what the other person needs and wants. You must understand what gets that person motivated or what his "hot button" is, as some sales people call it.

Get Advance Information

One way to do this is to get advance information. How? You can ask people who know the prospect, or observe for yourself. Information from others is especially appropriate if you are working with referrals or showing your product or service to people you already know. A secretary or receptionist can be an excellent source of information.

If your prospect has brochures and promotional materials, look through them. See what he is doing and think how your service or product might help.

Ask Questions

Questions are a key part of selling. You do not want simply to tell the prospect what you are offering. You want to know what that person wants, so you can tailor your presentation accordingly. This way you can focus your presentation on what is appropriate for that customer—or determine if you should be making it at all. If you have a product or service the customer does not want or need, and probably still won't want or need after you have made your best pitch, why do it? A better use of your time is to find a customer who is more likely to buy.

FIVE KEYS TO SUCCESSFUL SELLING

There are five stages of a sales transaction: get attention, build interest, develop conviction, encourage desire, and close with a call for action.

Get Attention

Once you have created rapport and qualified your prospect, get your prospect's attention by zeroing in on benefits. Your initial approach is critical. You have about four to ten seconds to make an impression and get the prospect's attention. One way to do this is provide attention-grabbing information that shows the value of your product and establishes credibility.

Build Interest: Match Needs to Benefits

Stress benefits, not product functions. Whenever someone is considering buying, he or she is thinking, "What is the value to me?" not "How does it work?" Don't go off track by only explaining how it works and why. Also describe its benefits. For example, if you are selling a word processing service, say:

> We specialize in meeting your deadlines, and we guarantee accuracy. You can choose the type styles to suite your purpose.

Do not say:

> We use a laser printer that prints 150 characters per minute, and we have a spelling checker on the system. We have 25 different type faces.

Note that both statements offer the same information about the service. The first, however, tells the prospect what benefits him. If he is then curious to know how you do it, you can give him the technical spiel.

Use what you already know about the prospect and probe further during your presentation to determine how to orient your talk. Maybe your prospect is an avid music fan and you're selling a time management system. You might point out how the system will help him have more time for concerts. If you're talking to an executive who's extremely busy, you might emphasize the economic benefits of better time planning.

Develop Conviction: Describe Your Product or Service

This is the heart of your presentation, and again, think of benefits to the prospect rather than features. Include a discussion of how or why the products work or how you perform your service.

Don't get too detailed, unless the prospect asks questions. Some people will be satisfied to learn that the product or service worked for you and most other people who tried it. They are otherwise only interested in a general idea of the product.

Be flexible. Sense the depth of your prospect's interest and knowledge, and respond accordingly. This might include a powerful testimonial or two by users, a compelling claim by researchers, your experience in using the product, a statement about the company's fast growth, or a quick demonstration of the product or service.

As time allows, spice up your presentation with color brochures, anecdotes, more testimonials and demonstrations, photographs, slides, or videotapes of the product in use—anything to make it more convincing.

If you forget anything, don't be concerned. Your prospect will probably never know, since you are the expert. It is the overall feeling your presentation leaves that usually clinches the sale. If something is important enough, the prospect will ask about it, or you can mention it when you follow up later.

Know the facts and stick to them. Even though your presentation features only the highlights of your product or service, it is important to have a solid, detailed knowledge of the facts. You must be able to come up with the answers if your prospect asks for details. If you don't know, you will lose credibility.

For the same reason, don't make unrealistic claims. It can be tempting to do so, but don't. Some hype can give pizzazz to your product or service. If there is too much of it, you again lose credibility.   People may not believe you when you tout all sorts of revolutionary new benefits (unless, of course, you have some solid back-up). And if people use the product themselves, they will soon find out if what you claimed is true.

Discuss (very briefly) the company. Many people want to know exactly who's behind the product or service, so talk about why this is a good company with a good reputation. If there have been previous product successes or media publicity, mention them.

The idea is to talk about how solid and stable the company is, even if the company is only you. Some topics to cover include the company's history in the business, or your own track record, if you're just getting started.

Offer back-up support. In some programs, back-up support doesn't matter much to consumers, since after the sale they simply get the product or service, and your role in selling it is complete. Or they may expect to order directly from the company on future orders.

But in other cases, consumers may look to you for advice and assistance in using the product or service. This is particularly true in the case of products which require ongoing follow-up for proper use, such as computers, software, and information-processing systems.

Stimulate Desire

To implant a desire to buy what you are selling, you must get the prospect involved emotionally. Successful sales people use a number of techniques for doing this, based on what they feel will best appeal to the prospect.

Involve the senses. Let the prospect experience what you are selling through as many senses as possible. Besides talking about it and showing it, so that the prospect **hears** about and **sees** it, let the customer **touch** it, and if appropriate, **smell** and **taste** it. And let him or her **use** it, if possible.

One of the best examples of this technique I ever saw was a cooking demonstration for pots and pans. While the demonstrator spoke, the food was quietly cooking in several pans on a hot plate, and people could smell it as it cooked.

Then they were invited to come up to taste the food, hold the pots, and even chop up vegetables, so that they could truly experience what it would be like to own the cookware.

The price was high, yet at the end of the talk, several people were ready to sign up. They had experienced the cookware personally. Despite the cost, they felt it was worth having.

Appeal to an Active Need. Another method of stimulating desire is to appeal to the active one of the following five needs:

Self-actualization (creative expression and goal achievement).

Recognition, pride or self-esteem (includes a desire for accomplishment or wealth).

Belonging (includes romance, love, and affection).

Safety and security (includes a desire for comfort and ease).

Survival or self-preservation (includes making a living).

From bottom to top, these motivators form a hierarchy of importance.

According to the psychologist Abraham Maslow, every person seeks to satisfy primary needs first, followed by the higher-order needs. In other words, someone is not motivated by a desire for a corner office with a bay view if he or she is hungry or homeless.

Assess your prospect's location on this hierarchy, and emphasize the benefits of your product or service that would satisfy that need.

Answer Questions and Objections

Invite the prospect to ask questions, and try to answer them. This is the ideal way to flush out any objections that may be in the way of making a sale.

A prospect may object because of a desire for more information, or because of a need for reassurance that the product is really good or that buying is the right thing.

Be ready. Answering objections effectively means being ready. If you are just starting out, take notes on the objections you hear so you can be ready for each one the next time you hear it. Notice how people respond to your answers, so you can keep the ones that work.

Acknowledge each objection respectfully. Then turn it around to show how it is really an advantage. Or move past it quickly to stress a benefit that is more important. Or ask why the prospect feels that way, if you think the feeling is not that strong or is based on incorrect facts. Be calm and confident.

Be persistent. People sometimes raise objections to test you, or simply as a knee-jerk response to a sales approach. You must plunge through this barrier by showing that you believe in what you are selling. If you persist and appear sincere and knowledgeable, they will usually agree to listen.

If the prospect still wants time to think it over, set up another meeting or suggest a time for you to call back. The idea is to stay in control, if the possibility of a sale is still open.

Don't argue. Remember, the customer is always right even when wrong. If your prospect seems sincerely hesitant, don't be too pushy. Instead, give the person some descriptive literature and possibly some samples to take home. And if it's appropriate, say you will be in touch to follow up. Don't leave that crucial follow-up decision to the prospect. Take the initiative yourself and call.

Finally, just accept it if your prospect doesn't like your product or service. Not everyone is going to like it, and if your prospect isn't convinced after hearing your presentation and answers to questions, you do not have to keep struggling.

As long as you gave the presentation your best shot, that's all you can do. Accept the fact that different people have different likes and interests, learn what you can from the experience (for example, how to polish your presentation to make it better), and go on to someone else.

Closing the Sale

A sales effort should be focused on creating value in the mind of the potential buyer, so that he or she wants your product or service. Then, once that person perceives that value, you have the basis for closing the sale. If it seems appropriate, ask for the order. Take out an application or order blank and urge the person to order or sign up now.

To close successfully, you must be aware that the person is ready to act. Look for appropriate "buy signals," which include such positive questions as, "When would I be able to get delivery?" or such positive comments as, "This really sounds good."

Trial closes. You may need to try closing more than once. Many sales people know, especially in making a major sale, that they will have to try closing three to five times. Thus, as you try each close, don't take "no" as necessarily final. You are using the trial closes to guide the prospect closer to assent. As you go along, you are zeroing in on what the person really needs and wants, so you can make the final close.

Offer incentives to order now. Sometimes it can help to offer a money-back guarantee to convince a person "to try it now." Once the person has parted with money, even with a guarantee, he or she has an incentive to try it out. Very few people ask for their money back.

However, I recommend not offering free sample trials. It can be easy to get a "yes" to a free offer, but the prospect may not really care about the product. A free sample of something else as a premium, on the other hand, can be a good idea to get a wavering prospect to buy.

Make it easy to reorder. Once you conclude a sale, explain how to place additional orders or say when you will call back for reorders. Remember, you are not concluding a one-time transaction, you are creating a relationship that will open the door to sales again and again. Once you have sold a person, you will find it much easier to sell that person again, so long as your product or service is good.

Ask for referrals. Always ask for referrals to other prospects. Mention categories of people who might be interested in your product or service, since this helps people recall names and phone numbers. For example, ask if they have friends, neighbors, business associates, members of groups they belong to who might be interested. After you mention each type, give them time to think. Get as much information as you can, including name, phone number and address.

4
Finding Leads

TARGETING YOUR MARKET

The first step in identifying prospective customers is to make a list of all potential categories of users. Next establish priorities of most likely users by rating the categories from 1 (least important) to 5 (most important).

Use the accompanying chart to help you establish the prime or target market for your products or services. The chart is divided into two sections: types of individuals (teenagers, children, mothers), and types of groups or businesses (health clubs, department stores, singles groups), who are most likely to use your products or services.

Rating   **Comments**

Types of individuals
most likely to use
products/services

Types of groups
most likely to use
products/services

List as many types of individuals and groups as you can, then rate them from 1 to 5 to indicate those most likely to use your products or services. For example, in selling a product to end users through personal presentation, in-home demonstrations and programs for groups, you will focus on individuals and informal groups.

A list for a weight-control products might look something like this:

Types of individuals: overweight people, mothers, and single people.
Types of groups: health clubs, weight-watcher groups, singles organizations, PTAs, and people in other diet programs.

In selling services to small businesses, you should focus on the types of businesses most interested in using your services. For instance, if you offer graphics services, you might skip individuals and list categories of businesses as follows:

Types of businesses: advertising agencies, department stores, boutiques, architectural firms, and banks.

In selling products, toys for example, your list might include toy wholesalers, toy stores, toy sections of department stores, stationery stores, variety stores, exhibitors of toys at fairs, and so on.

SOURCES FOR LEADS

Once you have identified the target market for your products or services, you are ready to make a systematic list of specific leads. There are many publications available to help you do this. Go through appropriate directories which you may have at home or at your library.

Directories

If you're looking for individuals as prospective customers, go through your personal telephone book, business card files, and membership lists of groups you belong to, combining all of the names on one master list. If you're trying to locate businesses, look through publications like Standard Rate and Data and yellow-page directories for neighboring counties at your library.

Specialized directories are often available from trade organizations and from publishers. Your local chamber of commerce may have a directory of members, the Better Business Bureau a membership roster, the phone company a business buyer's guide. The trade industry you are concerned with probably has a trade association directory.

Individuals

An efficient way to list leads is to begin with potential categories of users listed earlier. Within each category list specific names. If you're contacting individual end-users, some of the categories to use for specific names include:

Referrals.
Relatives.
Neighbors.
Old friends.
School friends.
Current friends.
Work associates.
Fellow commuters.
Merchants or clerks at stores where you shop.
People you meet at parties, classes, seminars, workshops.
Members of groups you belong to, such as church, social, interest, community, and service.
People whose services you use, such as doctors, dentists, hairdressers, mail carriers, repair people, gas-station attendants.

Groups

Other important sources of individual end-users are lists of special groups, as well as lists of well-connected individuals who are members of large networks of people.

Heads of groups are especially good to contact, because if they like your product or service, they can readily let their whole group know about it. Groups with wide contact networks include:

Schools.
Singles groups.
Political/civic groups.
Senior citizen groups.
Churches and temples.
Other religious groups.
Entrepreneurs' groups.
Insurance and real estate agents.
Local business networking groups.
Homeowner associations and tenant groups.
Youth groups, such as Boy Scouts, Girl Scouts.
Activity clubs, such as sports clubs, travel clubs.
Self improvement groups, such as Toastmasters.
Community service clubs, such as the Lions, Rotarians, fraternal lodges, and women's service groups.

Organizations and Businesses

If you're contacting organizations and businesses, some of the categories to use might be:

Referrals.
Churches.
Labor organizations.
Neighborhood stores.
Retail establishments.
Nonprofit associations.
Printers and typesetters.
Small businesses/offices.
Sports and recreational clubs.
Professionals in private practice.
Real estate and insurance businesses.
Health, educational and social institutions.
Specialty shops (boutiques, travel and luggage shops, sports stores, camera shops, computer stores).

This list is more open ended, since the types of organizations and businesses you contact will depend strongly on your type of product and the nature of your target market.

Preparing Lead Lists

Initially, list everyone you can think of. You never know who might be a good prospect until you ask. As before, maximize your efficiency by rating the people you plan to contact. Use 1 for the strongest possibilities through 5 for the poorest.

When you are ready to concentrate on a particular category (say churches or corporations), use the Lead Contact Sheet shown here to record the names of specific individuals, organizations, or businesses in that category. As you contact people, keep a record on either a single form like the Lead Contact Sheet, or on a separate Lead Contact Card (also shown) for each person or group.

A personal computer to keep track of leads is even better. With a computer file, it is much easier to pull out the names you want to contact, transfer them from one category to another, drop names into an inactive file, change names and addresses as people move, make notes of responses, and all the other tasks associated with keeping a leads list up to date.

Referrals should be noted on your Lead Contact Sheet or Card, so you can mention the name of the person who referred you when you make a contact. You can also use the Referrals chart given here for keeping all of your referrals together.

Lead Contact Sheet

	Date	Name/Address/Zip	Phone	Ref. by
1.				
2.				
3.				

	Send Info?	Set up meeting?	Result	Comments
1.				
2.				
3.				

Lead Contact Card

Name:
Address:
City/State/Zip:
Phone:
How Referred:
Program(s) Described:

Contact Dates	Interest?	Meeting?	Results?

Referrals

	Date	Name/Address/Zip	Phone	Ref. by
1.				
2.				
3.				

KEEPING RECORDS

Records are vital to effective selling. They provide a priority list of contacts. Also, they help you keep track of each contact, when you made it, and the response. Good records give a clear picture of who is interested and who is not. They tell you who to contact again, when, and about what.

Whenever you make contacts, note what people say. Are they interested or not? Do they want you to send information? Do they want you to call again? Should you make an appointment? Should you mail material, then follow up with a call? When should you take each step?

Each time you call, meet with someone, or send material, make a note so you can keep track of everything you do from initial contact to sale. After you have made a sale, indicate in your records what and how and when you should follow up.

Making Files

To stay on top of things, it helps to keep an active file of people and organizations you plan to contact within the next few days. You may want to create a tickler file by calendar day, indicating the contacts you are going to make each day. For instance, if a contact is interested and asks you to call back, note this on an index card and put it in your file under the appropriate day.

Computers are ideal for this kind of memory jogging. However, you can also do this by hand. Simply move information to the appropriate place in your file. Or you can make an extra copy of everything, using one set as the master file with all your leads and contacts filed alphabetically or by category. Copies of information you are actively working with can go into your active or tickler file.

When a contact says no, mark this on the card, explaining when and why and place it in an inactive file. Later when you have a new product or promotion that might appeal to this person, you can reactivate the card.

Records Help Improvement

Records are useful for learning how to improve. For instance, if you notice that a number of people give the same reasons for saying no, maybe there's something you can do to change that. Perhaps you are going after a wrong category of prospect; if so, think about how you might change.

Just because someone says no once, doesn't mean a no the next time. Needs may change, or next time you may have a better approach. If you keep good records, you will know what you should do when you try again.

GETTING REFERRALS

Whenever you talk to people about your product or service, ask them for referrals to other prospects, as appropriate. A person who buys the product or service you're offering may know someone else who would be an equally good customer. Or if they're not interested, they might know someone who is.

When you call, try to get at least three referrals and make a note of special comments, such as a personal interest in boats. Be sure to record the source of each referral, because when you mention a name, people are much more willing to listen. Referrals are like a key to a door. If these people are not interested, ask them for referrals too. In this way, you have an ever-expanding network of people to contact.

Later, when you organize a sales group, you can refer these names to your sales people. You'll find it's a real selling point for people who are considering selling your product if you can offer them hand-picked leads.

Use the referrals chart to keep track of referrals. Then, when you contact someone who is interested, transfer the name to your list of active prospects.

5
Using the Telephone Effectively

Many products and services are sold through presentations to individuals or groups, on the phone or in person. Your goal in using the telephone is to arouse people's interest in looking at information on your products or services, or in having a meeting with you. This chapter will help you polish your phone techniques to make an effective sales presentation.

Researchers studying the behavior of people meeting for the first time find that they decide within the first four seconds whether to continue their conversation. When you pick up the phone to make a sales call, you have only a few seconds to make a good first impression, with your voice alone. You must know exactly what you are going to say. Your very first words have to be right on target, or the person you call may hang up.

KEY STEPS IN PHONE SELLING

When you call, think of yourself as a stage director, with a play in three acts. Start with the right attitude by opening the conversation with a good lead, Act One. Keep the conversation going effectively, Act Two. End with a good close, Act Three. An excellent performance will pay off at the box office with a return engagement or a sale.

In most cases, your first call is designed only to open the door, so don't try to complete the sale on the phone. Unless you already know the person you call, you normally can't close a sale on the phone. People, particularly strangers, need to see something concrete, such as sales literature or the product. Your first call is meant to make them want to learn more.

Put Yourself in the Right Mood

Start with the right attitude. Not only what you say, but how you say it is critical. You've got to convey an enthusiastic, positive attitude. By showing excitement about your product or service, you will arouse your prospects' interest and make them more willing to listen to what you have to say.

Sometimes when you have a lot of calls to make or feel down, it's hard to generate the enthusiasm you need. Take a few moments to get yourself into a confident and calm state of mind. You can visualize being excited as you talk, and hearing the prospect respond positively.

Review What to Say

Have a general idea, in advance, of what you want to say. Start with a basic script or outline of the information you plan to cover. In this way you will have your lead-in and your major points already prepared. Modify them as the need arises.

Before you call review your presentation, and be ready to slant it toward the interests of the person you call. In this way your presentation is directed, yet spontaneous. You guide the conversation to your goal, while finding out what the other person wants.

Open with a Good Lead

Explain briefly who you are (if the person doesn't know you). Describe succinctly how your products or services will benefit the prospect.

It's important to state your professional credentials right away to establish credibility. You can reinforce this by speaking in an authoritative tone. You might say, "Hello. I'm Jan Allen of Word Plus. We have special business software packages that will help your company become more efficient and save money."

Say something catchy, even startling, to get attention. You can do this with a statement or with a question. "How would you like to cut your gas bills by 50%?" or, "I'm calling to tell you about a way you can cut your gas bills by 50%."

Focus Your Presentation

Once you've gotten the person's attention with a strong lead, get to the point quickly to keep it going smoothly. No one likes rambling calls or calls that begin with a number of unexplained questions. Establish your purpose quickly.

Focus on one or two key products or services. Group your basic information into one or two sentences or emphasize a few selected products or services which you feel have the most appeal.

You may have dozens of products or services to offer, but it is best to keep your phone presentation simple. This way you avoid confusing or overwhelming people. It's the same principle used in advertising: one main message creates the strongest impact.

Qualify Your Prospect

It's important to "qualify" your prospect. This involves asking questions to make sure the person is interested in your product or service, and that the product is appropriate. Through this qualifying, you determine if your product or service will meet these needs. Don't waste your time sending literature or setting up an appointment with someone who obviously isn't a candidate for your product, or who can't afford to pay for it.

List Key Benefits

List the key benefits of your product or service in order of importance on your outline. Start with your strongest suit first. If you encounter objections, either try to overcome them or skip to the next key benefit.

If the program has any special features that make it stand out, be sure to mention them. For instance, if you've got testimonials by name people, that's a plus. Celebrity names pack real power.

Another good way to add appeal is to vividly describe your product or service, so others can easily visualize it. This makes your products come alive. Say you're promoting a weight-control product. You might enthusiastically say:

It's a fantastic health program, endorsed by dozens of doctors and medical professionals. You drink these terrific-tasting drinks that look and taste like malts, exercise about a half hour a day, and listen to tapes that help you see yourself thin. And it works. Most of the people on the program lose about three pounds a week.

Don't Go into Too Much Detail

Remember, your goal is to get potential customers interested in seeing your literature or setting up an appointment. Don't go into a lot of detail over the phone. Stay in control of the conversation.

Use your script or outline to help you do this. If people ask for more details, simply explain that you're sending them detailed information, or that you need to meet with them personally to go into more detail. In this way, you keep your calls short and don't waste time.

End with a Good Close

After you've gotten your message across, wind up with a statement or request for action. It might be something like this:

> Good. Then, I'll go ahead and send you some material and call next week. How do you spell your name? Also, let me get your address. In the meantime, if you decide you would like to place an order, please call collect, or use our postpaid order form.

Make a note to follow through on promised call-backs.

Ask for Referrals

If people aren't interested in your products or services themselves, they may know someone who is. Be specific. Mention a particular type of product benefit, and ask if they know a person who might be interested in that benefit. This helps them think of people they know, whereas a general question is more likely to draw a blank.

For instance, if you were selling a diet program, you might ask, "Do you know someone who would be interested in losing five to ten pounds a month?"

Or in the case of consulting services, you might say, "Do you know any other small business people who would be interested in a computer consultant who can help them set up a more efficient system?"

USING THE PHONE TO SET UP SALES APPOINTMENTS

If you are using the telephone to arrange a face-to-face meeting, there are several guidelines that will smooth the way in setting up an effective meeting.

Ask for a Firm Commitment

Make it clear when you set up the appointment that the time and place are definite and ensure that the other person understands this. Often people will say, "I'll try to make it," or "I'll let you know." Unfortunately, such tentative arrangements frequently fall through.

If a person sounds uncertain about making a commitment, stress that you are planning on a definite appointment and plan to be there. You might say something like, "Okay, I'm writing this down in my calendar now. We'll be meeting together at (name the time and place), and I'll be counting on seeing you then."

To stress the importance of the meeting and your willingness to fit the person into your busy schedule, you might say, "Okay, I've got your meeting blocked out for (name the time and place). If something should come up, please give me plenty of notice, so we can reschedule our appointment. My time slots usually fill very quickly."

Limit Available Times

When you first suggest the meeting, limit the available times the person can attend. This helps to pin people down. Avoid asking prospects when they can make a meeting. Instead, name a few times you have available, or give them a choice of two or three days and ask which they would prefer. It's easier to get people to say yes or no to your suggestions than it is to get them to think through their schedules to suggest possible meeting times.

If people agree to appointments and then cancel them at the last minute, put them off for the next meeting. This way, prospects won't think you are available any old time. If they have to wait, it may convince them that an appointment with you is valuable; that it's worth waiting for.

Emphasize the Importance of the Meeting

If people agree to a meeting, emphasize how important the meeting will be and let them know that their presence matters to you. In some sales programs, you may invite people to group presentations. If so, be sure to make each person feel his or her presence is important.

In a group meeting, people often feel they have the option of showing up or not, and may not make a decision until the last minute. Point out that you care if they show up.

For example, say something like, "Okay, I'm making a reservation for you for our meeting on (time and place). I want to be sure you know we can only take a limited number of people at our meetings. So if something should come up, please give me plenty of notice, so I can invite you to another meeting."

Offer Transportation

If the meeting is at a location other than your office or the person's own office, take the person to the meeting, rather than meet there, if possible. Such an offer is good for several reasons. First, you score points for your consideration.

Second, you make it convenient for the person to look at your product or service. This will make most people feel obligated to attend and personally important, because you are going out of your way for them.

Once a prospect indicates an interest in going with you, make it clear this is a firm arrangement, and arrange logistics. Say something like, "Okay, I'll pick you up at (time and date), and we'll go to the meeting together. I'm putting this on my calendar now, and I'll see you then. Be sure to let me know if you need to make any changes."

Confirm Appointments

Confirm appointments that were set up more than a day or two earlier. This reduces the risk of no-shows. When you call to confirm, don't ask if the person still plans to attend. That gives people a chance to rethink their interest in the meeting and product. Instead, act on the assumption of continued interest, and simply say you are calling to confirm the time and place of the meeting.

Begin with a few comments that will encourage enthusiasm such as, "I'm calling to confirm our meeting for tomorrow. We've just announced a few new products, so this should be a really productive meeting." Briefly restate your agreed-upon arrangements, such as, "We'll see you in our offices at twenty-two Webster Street on the ninth floor," or "I'll pick you up at your house at forty-five Allen Street at eight a.m."

If people ask questions about your program, cut them off firmly and politely. Questions will only encourage them to reconsider. Instead, say that people will have plenty of opportunity to ask questions at the meeting.

If people say they can't make it, probe a little to find out why, and if they seem sincerely interested, reschedule the meeting. Mention that you are quite busy, but will squeeze them in.

Dealing with Lack of Enthusiasm. If you feel the prospect is cancelling because of uncertainty about the product, simply say you are sorry they can't make it and that they will be missing a valuable opportunity. For example, "Oh, that's too bad, since we'll be ending our 25% discount program at the end of the week." (In some cases, you'll find that people who are wavering may decide to keep appointments after all, at this point.)

When you do reschedule an appointment with someone who seems to lack enthusiasm, say that you can't schedule the meeting for a week or two because of other commitments. This shows you aren't pushy. As before, give them a limited choice of times.

Sending Confirming Notes. Another approach is to send out a confirming note to remind the prospect of the time and place of an appointment that was made more than a week in advance. A written confirmation has a certain air of authority, and people are less likely to say no to it. Also, such a confirmation reinforces the importance of the occasion. I have found the results to be about the same, whether calling or writing. I prefer the personal touch of calling. Use the approach that feels comfortable for you.

No-Shows: Follow Up or Ignore?

Even with the best of appointment-setting techniques, some prospects will not appear. Sales people have different ways of responding. Some drop no-shows from their lists. Others call to find out why the prospect did not show up. Personally, I prefer to skip the follow-up call and go on to other people. To evaluate what works best for you, review your track record in follow-up calls compared to calling new prospects.

If the prospect sounded genuinely interested in the original conversation, call back to find out what happened. Be upbeat. Give a capsule review of what they missed. Do not to put people on the spot about why they didn't come. That only makes them defensive and discourages interest in your product. By contrast, a positive call with new information might trigger another meeting and a sale.

6
Effective Presentations

Your presentation can make or break your sale. A good sales person knows how to be sensitive to the prospect, yet stays in control of the conversation, and gradually builds up to an effective close, using the kind of sales techniques already described.

At this point, you have invested a lot of time in locating leads, making phone calls, sending out literature, and making appointments. You want to make sure that your presentation is a good one.

IDENTIFY THE RIGHT PERSON TO SEE

One of the first requirements of a successful presentation is to talk to the right person, something you should check on when you set up the appointment. You should be talking to the decision maker, the person who can say "yes" or "no." In some large companies, you may have to go through a series of presentations at lower levels of the company. But where you can, zero in on key decision makers with your presentation.

If there are several people involved in making a decision, make sure they are all at the presentation. For example, if you are trying to sell a product or service in someone's home and the prospect is married, be sure both husband and wife are present. This avoids the excuse, "I have to talk it over with my spouse first." The couple may still want to discuss and think about the purchase, but they are better able to decide.

Another approach is to expand from a one-on-one to a small group presentation involving three to six people. This is less expensive than a presentation to one or two people, and it avoids the danger of wasting an appointment on a no-show. In a meeting with several people, you spend your time more productively. Also, the small meeting format preserves the intimacy found in a one-on-one presentation.

PLANNING THE PRESENTATION

A second requirement for a good presentation is to be prepared. Plan in advance what you are going to say. In this way, you can keep your presentation short and to the point, which is more powerful. Also, build into your presentation a clear picture of what you want to cover and how you want to do it.

Preferably keep your presentation to about half an hour; otherwise, prospects may lose interest. On the other hand, if prospects have lots of questions it shows they are interested, and you can go longer.

Have supporting materials organized and close at hand, so you can readily refer to specific items in your presentation.

It is important to have your ideas and style of presentation organized. It is not enough just to have a general idea of what you want to say. You may forget major points and be haphazard in your coverage.

It is also important to have an outline or script for the presentation firmly in mind. You may want to write it out and assemble your supporting materials in the order in which you want to refer to them.

The checklists shown here can help you get organized. The Presentation Checklist will help you determine what items you need to have on hand and in what order you want to use them for the presentation. The Outline Guide will help in organizing your outline.

Once your basic organization is in place, practice the presentation until you are familiar with your major points and their sequence. If you prefer, refer to your outline or script (possibly on note cards or in your presentation binder) when you make your first presentations. In this way you are sure to cover your complete agenda and will feel more relaxed while doing it. Later, you will know the material by heart and won't need written material.

Presentation Checklist

Items to Use, in Order of Presentation	Have	Need
1.		
2.		
3.		

Outline Guide

Opening (initial statement/opening remarks)

1.
2.
3.

Main Topics to Cover (list both key topics and main subpoints)
1.
2.
3.

Possible Objections to Expect and Prepare for
1.
2.
3.

Closing (list alternative closes to use)
1.
2.
3.

USING SUPPORTING MATERIALS

Supporting materials are useful for creating interest and providing proof that you represent a good company with good products or services. They contribute to the success image you want to create.

Handouts

It is a good idea to have a packet of materials to hand out after your presentation so that prospects can take them home to review. Include materials like brochures, question and answer sheets, order blanks, and flyers. This shows that your program is really solid and professional. Just giving out your business card is not enough.

While it's ideal to make the sale on the spot, some prospects will want to consider and review your offer. If so, it's important that they have something tangible to review, which reminds them of the major benefits discussed in the presentation.

You may want to include additional supporting documents not mentioned in your presentation, such as testimonials from satisfied product users or information on how or why the product works (which is particularly important if you have a health or nutrition product or a high-tech product).

Presentation Book

A presentation book allows you to go over major points of your presentation in a step-by-step fashion as you flip from page to page. This helps you stay on target and avoid forgetting major points. Also, you can readily adapt a manual for different presentations by shifting sections around in response to your prospect's interest.

Graphs, Charts, and Posters

Visual aides can make your presentation more solid and interesting. They're also good for graphically showing the points you make. You can display them on a flip chart or on the wall. at the appropriate moment.   If they are small enough, you can put them into your presentation book.

Testimonials

The source of testimonials is important.   Depending on the circumstances, use testimonials from people who commonly use your products or services, from people of different types to show that interest in your product is broadly based, or select people who are similar to your prospect.

This latter type of testimonial is especially important, because it helps the prospect more closely identify with the people using your program. If you can, present this type of testimonial first. You can use either tapes or letters (videotapes if you have them).

If you use testimonial letters, they should be on a nice-looking letterhead. Include identifying material about the person giving the testimonial if it's not already provided in the letter or tape. List name, town, occupation, and how long this person has been a consumer or user of your services.

Slides or Videos

If you have the budget, use slide-sound, slide-script or video presentations that are professionally produced. They can be slick and impressive. Alternatively, if you feel creative, you can add a personal touch to your presentation by producing your own show or by adding some of your own slides or tapes to a company-produced presentation. For example, show yourself or some friends using the product or service.

MAKING THE PRESENTATION

As you prepare to make your presentation, keep in mind the five building blocks of sales: attention, interest, conviction, desire, and close. Also be aware of the need to emphasize benefits and create value.

Within this framework, do your presentation in the way that feels best for you. If you are using a presentation book and have supporting materials, arrange them to follow the same sequence, so your presentation flows easily.

Depending on your program, vary the sequence in which you make your presentation to emphasize the benefits you feel will most appeal to that prospect.

Start with something interesting to get your prospect's attention, the first step in selling anything. Then build interest by showing how the prospect's needs are filled by the benefits of the product or service. Next, work on arousing the desire to buy your product or service.

When questions or objections arise, use this as an opportunity to increase your prospect's confidence by providing good answers. Finally, help your prospect make a decision and take action by showing that this action will be beneficial and produce satisfaction.

If possible, encourage the prospect to act at once. But if someone hesitates and is unwilling to decide right away, allow time to review your product or service, providing additional information as necessary to help in the decision.

7
Recruiting Others to Sell For You

Once you have had experience in selling your own product or service, and what you offer has a proven track record, you are ready to recruit others to sell for you. There are advantages if you begin by signing up established commission sales representatives or brokers who have their own sales network.

These people are already experienced in sales, minimizing the amount of training required. Then your job becomes primarily coordinating your sales network and providing back-up support through promotional and sales materials.

COMMISSION SALES REPRESENTATIVES

In just about every industry you'll find a commission sales rep or broker to handle your product or service. Typically, they work on a 10-15% commission, occasionally as much as 20%, depending on the type of product, how many products you have, how long you have been in business, your previous track record, and how much they want to carry your item.

With high-volume items like toys, commissions tend to be lower, about 10%. With specialty items having a higher markup and fewer sales per order, commissions are a little higher; about 15% is average.

However, when you have only a few products, are new in business, or have an untested product, you may end up paying a little more. When you are starting out, you need reps more than they need you, and the higher commission they are likely to ask for reflects this fact.

Sales Support

Commission reps normally need only a few product samples or catalog sheets and price lists from you to go out and sell. You don't need to do anything else. But it helps if you do.

For example, if you or your product has received publicity, let the reps know and provide them with a sheet showing the clippings or a collage of clippings.

Also, if a rep is going to attend a trade show, you can help by being there to call attention to your product or demonstrate it to potential buyers. Trade shows also give you a chance to talk with reps from other areas who attend the show.

Exclusive Territories

Individual sales reps usually cover exclusive territories. For example, a rep may cover the San Francisco Bay Area, Northern Illinois, or the entire state of Pennsylvania. They may even cover several states. Also, they usually call on specific types of businesses such as toy stores and toy departments, gift and stationery buyers, boutiques and clothing stores.

This leaves you free to work with reps in other territories or in other sales niches. However, anything sold in an area where a rep has exclusive representation, including direct sales by you (unless there is a special exemption for selected house accounts), is credited to the rep in paying a commission.

Frequently one rep will recommend reps to cover other territories, allowing you quickly to put together a national sales network.

Agreements

Agreements with sales reps may be only temporary, made for a selling season beginning in January, or whenever the rep is hired, and running through December. Commonly there is a mutual cancellation clause allowing either you or the rep to end the arrangement with a 30-day written notice. The rep normally gets a commission for sales initiated before the end of the agreement if he or she closes the sale, or if the customer pays soon after the agreement ends.

HOW TO SELECT A GOOD REPRESENTATIVE

One way to find a rep when you're just getting started is to go to a trade show featuring products similar to yours. Walk up and down the aisles until you see someone with a product line of similar items.

Another way to find a rep is to visit a local merchandise mart where there are reps for your kind of product. Alternatively, contact local stores where you would expect your product to sell and ask to speak to the appropriate buyer. Ask for suggestions about reps who might handle your product.

After talking with a few buyers, you'll find that some reps are mentioned again and again. Call some of them, especially those who have been mentioned frequently, and set up interviews. Ask questions important to selecting a good rep for your products. All things being equal, you may want to choose those reps who are mentioned the most.

Besides asking about territory coverage and the types of accounts handled, you also want to find out about sales reps' backgrounds and how enthusiastic they are about your product. And, of course, you want to know the expected commission.

Major Considerations

Following are several questions to ask yourself in selecting a good sales rep to sell your product.

How well will my product fit in with the rep's other products? It should fit, though it shouldn't be directly competitive with another product. For example, if you have games, it's ideal to find a rep who handles other games. But if you both have games on money, the match may be too close. Many reps will turn you down if they feel the products are too directly competitive.

Are the products the rep currently has of high quality and from good manufacturers? The answer should be yes. If the rep represents some solid established companies, that's a sign of a good reputation. Also, your products will benefit by their association with other high-quality, well-known products.

Can the rep adequately represent my product? You want to be sure the rep will really push your product and give it a good shot. Sometimes this means a rep with a smaller line may be better for you when you're just getting started. With a larger line your product might get lost among all of the others. In other cases, a rep with a larger and better established line may have better customer connections.

What kind of track record does the rep have? How long has the rep been in business? Or if he just started his own firm, how long has he worked for someone else in the field? When a rep is already handling several established product lines, this is probably not an issue. But if a rep's line is relatively small, you want to be sure of experience. Reps must know what they are doing.

How well will a rep's territory and types of accounts fit in with those of other reps in my network? This type of fit is important if you are trying to set up a regional or national sales network, because you want to avoid conflicts over territory and accounts.

In some cases, reps will compromise over overlaps in their outlying territories, so you can accommodate reps who both handle the same area. One might agree not to include a certain territory, or both might agree to non-exclusive coverage there.

Try to avoid such conflicts where you can. Using referrals from the reps you already have can be one way to avoid this problem, because they will usually recommend people who have nonconflicting territories.

How well does the rep like my product? It's much better to choose a rep who really likes it, than one who's only lukewarm. The first rep will really work for you; the other will typically just add your product to see how it flies. Most products don't sell themselves. They depend on someone pushing them, and here a good rep is the key to good sales.

WORKING WITH A SERVICE BROKER

Service brokers or agents are a little like employment agencies representing a particular type of service. Typically, they are local, and solicit customers for your service. Sometimes they have national connections as well.

Often brokers represent just one service, such as writing, speaking, graphics, or the performing arts. But there are many general business brokers, too, who represent people with varying business skills such as word processing, accounting, bookkeeping, or public relations.

Service brokers differ from employment or temporary service agencies in that they represent your business, which provides the services.

Commission Percentages

You usually cannot count on service brokers for more than a percentage of your sales. But they can supplement what you and your sales people are already doing. Your relationship to them is that of an independent contractor. They take a percentage from either you or the customer they find for you. Depending on the industry, this can range from about 10% to 50%. Some service brokers have set fees, and others will negotiate.

How it Works

As an example of how these services work, many speakers use a speakers' bureau to represent them. In fact, most speakers work with several bureaus in different parts of the country. Where there are several bureaus in an area, there is no exclusivity, so speakers often list with more than one. In that case, the bureaus ask each speaker to be consistent so various brokers can ask the same fee for that speaker.

In most cases, speakers get only about 10% of their business through bureaus. They book the rest of their business directly. However, these extra sales from brokers can be substantial. Many bureaus offer product sales as well, so that speakers receive additional royalty or product income from their books, videos, and cassettes.

Where to Look

Where do you find service brokers? One source is your local yellow pages. Look under the type of business you have. You will probably find companies that offer their own services, as well as brokers who offer them. Check trade publications for broker advertising, and your local chamber of commerce directory of business services.

Still another source for finding service brokers is business network meetings. Brokers often come out in force for these meetings, since they are a potential source of new clients. In fact, if you leave a brochure or flyer on your services at such gatherings, you'll find that brokers will frequently contact you.

8
Recruiting a Sales Manager

When the time comes for you to build your own sales force, you may decide to act as sales manager yourself while you recruit and work with sales people, until you find someone who can take over. Also, it may be necessary for you to act as sales manger for a while in order to get your product on the market. Once your product has a track record, it is easier to get someone else to take over.

On the other hand, if you prefer to play only a minor role in organizing a sales group, you must recruit a good sales or marketing manager. How do you find a good sales manager, and what incentives should you offer?

WHERE TO FIND A SALES MANAGER

There are two key sources to consider in searching for a sales manager: advertising and professional organizations.

Advertising

To advertise for sales people, your local newspaper classifieds are ideal. A local business daily is also excellent. List your ad under Sales Management or Sales Manager.

For certain specialties, such as computer software or financial services, list the industry first and then sales management. People interested in special fields will look under the industry heading first.

What to say in the ad. Briefly describe your product or service and what type of selling or management is required. Note whether you are paying a commission only or a commission and draw, and tell what kind of background is expected. For example: "Sales Management. Gift products. Must be experienced in direct sales. Sell to companies, organizations. Comm. only. Call (number)."

It's important to be specific, and state qualifications and commission arrangements. Such screening in the ad reduces the number of inappropriate calls. When people call, be prepared to do some additional screening on the phone, as well as give details about the job.

What to say when people call. You can cut down the time you talk to callers and can be more efficient in meetings if you are prepared for calls in response to the ad. For example, prepare a brief outline or script of whatever you plan to tell callers and questions you plan to ask. Respond with a sentence or two telling specifically what the job entails, then ask callers to tell you a little about their own backgrounds in sales.

If you decide that a person has the right qualifications, set up an interview. For a sales manager's position, interview one person at a time.

Professional Organizations

You may find local organizations of sales people or organizations whose members have sales backgrounds. Some of these groups even have job files where you can search for a sales manager. National organizations which may have a chapter near you include Association of Sales and Marketing Executives and National Association of Professional Sales Women.

Also, your chamber of commerce may sponsor business networking events or provide a directory of people in different fields. Other local sources include leads clubs, tips clubs, organizations for older business and professional people looking for work, such as 40-plus groups, and civic groups of business people, such as the Lions Club, Rotary Club, and Soroptimists.

WHAT TO LOOK FOR IN A SALES MANAGER

A sales manager who is going to hire other sales people must be good at leading and managing others. The person selected should have a good record of previous management experience, preferably in sales, and a few good references.

Look also for integrity and a strong ethical sense. Your sales manager is going to be setting the tone for other sales people in how your product or service is presented to customers. For long-term growth, integrity and ethical behavior are crucial.

The Right Fit

You need someone who reflects your own style of doing business. You need someone who is going to represent you and your vision of what the company should be. In a sense, your sales manager is an extension of you and provides a role model for other sales people in your company. So choose carefully. You can usually trust your gut-level sense.

Some other aspects to note are appearance, style, and personality. Choose a person with the qualities properly to represent you and your product. If you are polished, urbane, and sophisticated and your product or service appeals to people of this kind, then choose a sales manager with a similar image. Conversely, if you and what you sell are more down-home and folksy, find someone who is down-home and folksy, too.

Finally, besides making sure that your sales manager has the basic qualities that contribute to success, make sure that the two of you work well together.

Personal Qualities

Look for the following personal qualities in your sales manager. When you talk to potential candidates, ask questions which will allow you to assess these qualities.

Hard working: Enjoys the challenge of doing a job well and putting in the hours necessary to see it through.

Competitive: Has entered competitions and won, and likes to take on new challenges.

Well organized: Has goals, a plan to achieve them, and is good at details and following through.

Takes initiative: Creative in coming up with new ideas and activities and in putting them into practice.

Willing to learn: Receptive to new information and techniques. Learns quickly.

Good track record: Has been successful in sales and management.

Good leader and teacher: Previously coached or taught others and directed and managed people.

Good motivator: Inspires others by word and example.

Good listener: Wants to hear what other people are interested in and need. (This is the key to good sales and to effective management of other people.)

Likes people: Crucial factor for anyone in selling or management.

Has positive, optimistic attitude: A must for anyone in selling or sales management. A sales leader has to be able to look constantly on the bright side and keep going. This helps keep other sales people optimistic and motivated, too.

HIRING A SALES MANAGER

In interviews, you have to make the job sufficiently appealing to recruit a good person. You should be able to answer the following questions in order to give prospective sales managers a clear picture of what opportunities are available. They must decide if there is enough return for them to do the job.

What are the major benefits of my product or service? How does it compare to the competition? What are its major selling features which can be used to make it easy to sell?

What kind of sales volume is likely? About how much time and effort are required to achieve that sales volume?

Shall I pay a commission only, or a commission draw? A draw is a minimum guaranteed commission. Commissions can be earned that exceed the draw.

What are the commission arrangements for personal sales? What kind of overrides and bonuses are available if the sales manager brings in other sales people?

Approximately how much is a person in this position likely to make, based on the commission offered and the likely sales volume in a given amount of time (such as 20 or 40 hours a week)?

Projected Sales Estimate

If your product or service does not have a track record of sales, you can work out a projected estimate, based on how others are doing with similar products. Then you can project your estimate by using the following steps:

List the number of expected or projected sales for each category of product or service.

Multiply the average monthly sales volume of each sales person by the value of each sale to get a total monthly sales value.

Sum the monthly sales values to get a total personal sales value.

List the average hours needed to achieve this monthly sales volume.

Multiply the total monthly sales value by the average commission on
personal sales.

Multiply the total monthly sales value per person by the number of
sales people expected to be supervised by the sales manager, and
then multiply by the manager's override bonus percentage.

Divide the average time needed to achieve this monthly sales volume
into the total projected earnings to get average pay per hour.

Commission Only or Draw?

You'll find it easier to recruit a sales manager if you offer a draw.
(Although if you're just starting, you may not be able to do this.)   Many
good sales people don't have the resources to work completely on
speculation. However, some of the very best sales people prefer a
commission-only arrangement since they can make more this way.

When a company seeks a straight-commission sales manager, its
commission offer will be somewhat more than a base salary or draw.
For instance, a common draw arrangement might be $2000 per month
against a 25% commission, versus 33% as a commission only.

You may want to offer a prospective manager the option of choosing
either one. But be sure that the manager is likely to sell enough to
make at least the amount of the draw when you offer that option.
Otherwise it won't work.

If you offer both options, note the reasons behind a choice. A
hotshot, confident sales person will take the commission-only
arrangement if it is likely to pay more. On the other hand, people
often have valid reasons for needing a draw, such as high personal
debts or a tight cash situation. Consider these reasons along with other
factors in deciding who you want in the job.

Trial Period

I recommend setting up arrangements on a 30- to 60-day trial basis. The
sales manager should get credit for any sales made or initiated during
that period, whether the arrangement becomes permanent or not.

During a trial period, you have time to assess each other and
decide if you want to continue to work together. In particular, you
should look at results. How have sales been during this period? Is your
sales manager effective in working with sales people and motivating
them?

CREATING A PARTNERSHIP

Before you begin looking for a sales manager, you should consider whether you want to hire a sales manager as an employee or as a co-owner of your business. In today's competitive environment, the role of the sales or marketing manager has become so important that an individual manager can sometimes make or break a company. Carefully consider which arrangement is best for you.

With the right person, a partnership can make a lot of sense if you're just starting off, don't have much money, and need someone to take over the sales/marketing function.

Constructing a Proposal

As part of your proposal to a prospective partner, you should also work out projections for earnings as best you can, just as in seeking to hire a sales manager. This will help a potential partner evaluate this opportunity and the possibilities for future growth.

To provide motivation, I suggest that you include some kind of commission plan as part of your partner's compensation, even though both of you will share the profits. In this way, there will be an immediate payoff tied to sales. If profit is far down the road, the partnership offer itself may not look as good.

Advertising

If you want to find a partner, your ad should go under Business Opportunities, rather than in the Help Wanted section. In fact, advertising under Business Opportunities you may even find someone to put up money for a share of the business. This would show real commitment. At least you may find someone willing to work on commission only in return for a share of the business.

As in a help-wanted ad, be specific about what you want the person to do, and note your partnership or commission offer. For example: "Partner with sales management background sought for small gift products business. Become sales manager. No investment req. Commission/Partnership arrangement. Call (number)."

As in advertising for employees, prepare your response to calls in advance. Give a few more details about your company, then find out whether the caller has the background and interest to fit well into your company.

Advantages and Arrangements

One advantage to a partnership is that you don't have to pay a partner in advance. You may even find a partner who is willing to invest in getting the business started.

The major caution in forming a partnership is to be sure you have the right person, since once the partnership is created you're locked in together. You can arrange a trial by setting up an agreement that is provisional for the first few months. Then, should you want it, the agreement makes it easy to split up.

If you do want a partner, think out in advance your respective roles and responsibilities and how you will split ownership. A 50-50 arrangement is common in partnerships, but the split depends on who does what. For example, if you're putting up the money as well as providing the product or the service, a 60-40 or 67-33 split may make more sense. Or perhaps allow for a sliding split based on how the company evolves.

In any case, it's a good idea to go over your proposed arrangements with a lawyer after you and your prospective partner reach a tentative agreement. In this way, you can avoid unexpected sticking points that otherwise may cause problems later on.

9
Recruiting Your Own Sales Team

When you hire sales people to work directly for you, particularly those who work on commission only, the kind of in-depth interviewing necessary in hiring a sales manager isn't needed. You need only look for those basic qualities that make a good sales person. Use a brief application form and hold a 5 to 15-minute interview.

If you are favorably impressed, offer the applicant a job on a trial basis for a few weeks to see how it works out. If the person can sell well, you'll see results in the form of sales or at least strong prospects.

If results are poor, terminate the arrangement. Anyone who performs poorly will likely be ready to leave. As you find out who is good at selling and who isn't, you can begin building your good people into a strong sales team.

GETTING READY TO RECRUIT

Before you begin recruiting, you should have your sales materials, such as flyers, brochures, and catalog sheets, already prepared so that you will be ready to answer questions when applicants call, and ready to put newly hired sales people to work.

How do you determine what kind of person you want? Do you want someone to work on commission only or will you pay a draw? The answers to these questions will affect how you advertise and recruit, and where.

What Kind of Person Do You Want?

Selecting the right kinds of sales people depends on the nature of your product or service, and the characteristics of the target markets.

How complex is it to sell your product or service? If extensive product knowledge (such as with a computer or high-tech product) or sales skills and training (such as with a beauty product that must be demonstrated) are required, an experienced person is needed. If little product knowledge is required, then people with limited or no sales background could sell it, as long as they have the people skills and personality that are essential in a good sales person.

Is the product or service directed toward a certain market, such as certain age groups, genders, lifestyles, income levels? If so, it's a good idea to find sales people who have similar characteristics as the target group. They will be better able to develop the rapport necessary to make a sale.

For products that appeal to college students, hire college students or young adults. For products that appeal to suburban housewives, hire women. If you want to hit the business and professional market, use men and women with previous business experience.

Certainly many sales people can cut across markets and sell to virtually anyone. But sales will be better generally if your sales people are like the people they are trying to sell.

How and How Much Should You Pay?

Should you pay a salary, possibly with bonuses? A commission with draw? Or a commission only? This depends on what you want to do and how much you can afford.

Salary. Normally, sales people work on either a straight commission or a commission with draw. But under certain circumstances, a salary might make sense. For instance, if you plan to do the follow-up and presentations to customers yourself, it might be helpful simply to hire someone to make the preliminary phone calls.

Or you might hire someone to go through an introductory script on the phone to set up appointments for a sales person to follow up later. You could pay such a person an hourly wage, possibly combined with a bonus for appointments that result in sales, perhaps 10% to 20% of the net amount of these sales.

Commission and draw. With a commission and draw arrangement, you have more control over your sales people than with a commission only. They are more like regular employees, and you can expect more of them, such as working a certain number of hours a week. Typically, such a system is used with unskilled sales people who are just learning the business. Since they are drawing a base wage, the commission rate is lower than it would be in a commission-only arrangement. Inexperienced sales people usually need a base wage because they can't afford to work on speculation. Their cash flow from sales isn't enough to live on. Also, they may lack the confidence of sales people willing to work on commission only.

Sometimes you may want sales people to do fairly routine work, such as make phone calls, go door to door, or operate a booth at a flea market or fair. All they need is base pay. But if you pay a commission it will provide an extra incentive to do well.

Commission only. You'll find that many of the best sales people, if they like your product, prefer an opportunity to make more on a commission-only arrangement. For example, the big earners in insurance, real estate, securities, travel, and many other fields all work this way. They work for you as independent contractors, free to choose their own hours. You can make your office available to them, but they may prefer to work out of their own homes.

In setting up a commission system, you should structure it to encourage sales people to get out and sell as much as possible. Assuming the pricing, costs and profit on your product or service allow it, you should keep the commission high. This way you will attract good, motivated sales people, resulting in more sales and profits.

A common commission arrangement for direct sales at full retail prices starts at around 25% of the retail price with added incentives, so that a top sales person can make as much as 40 to 60% on direct sales. In an override system, about 25 to 40% might go to the person who makes the sale and another 10 to 20% to the other sales people involved in sponsoring, supporting, and supervising.

RECRUITING THROUGH ADVERTISING

Once your sales materials and product literature are ready and you have decided on pay arrangements, the next step in recruiting is to advertise through your local newspaper or local sales and business organizations.

Before placing ads, it's important to plan in advance how you are going to handle the responses. When you advertise, you will get numerous calls, which must be screened.

Screening Calls

Many sales managers simply work up a brief explanation of their product or service and a description of the kind of sales people the company is looking for. They ask the caller a few questions and decide whether to arrange an interview.

Using a prerecorded phone message. If you don't have the time or inclination to deal with calls directly, use a recorded message or a special phone line. When people call, your message explains briefly what the position entails and what kind of person you are looking for. People who are interested can call another number to talk to you directly.

The advantage of this approach is it gets rid of callers who find that they aren't interested in applying. Moreover, when people who are interested call back, you don't have to spend a lot of time explaining the product or service. They have already heard about it. Instead, you can ask them a few questions to see if they are qualified. If they are, you can set up an appointment for an interview.

In my own experience, about 50% of the callers who listened to the recorded message hung up and didn't call again. Most of the rest who did call wanted to set up an appointment. Each time I used this system, I saved three or four hours of time on the phone.

If you're going to use a recording for screening, you don't have to say this in your ad. People will find out when they call. An ad that says, "call for recorded message" can put off potential callers, as well as make the ad cost more.

Using someone else to screen calls. If you don't like recordings but don't want to answer all of the calls yourself, you can hire someone to explain what the position offers and the qualifications required, using a brief script. Then interested callers can call back and speak to you.

Where to Advertise

Probably the most productive source of leads will be your local paper's Help Wanted section in the Sunday edition. Depending on the nature of your company, more specialized papers will also draw well. And, do not overlook job banks run by organizations for sales people.

Specialty papers. Besides your local daily paper, another good place to advertise certain types of products and services might be a local weekly, featuring local events and lifestyles. Most major cities have them, such as the San Francisco *Bay Guardian*, *The Village Voice* in New York, and the Los Angeles *Free Press*.

The job ads in these papers often feature unique sorts of work for small companies and are designed to appeal to people who are looking for alternative, out-of-the-ordinary kinds of jobs. If you have a product or service that appeals to such a group, this might be a good place to advertise. Check the help-wanted columns to see what kind of positions are being advertised. If your sales position fits in, it's probably a good bet your ad would pull well, too.

Job banks. Some organizations for sales people in your area may have a jobs bank or jobs coordinator where you can list your job opportunity. For example, a group called National Association of Professional Saleswomen lists jobs of interest to members, and they may have a chapter in your area.

Another possibility is self-help groups for older workers trying to find jobs. Many of these people are very competent, experienced and eager for work. And, a part-time or short-term sales job might be very attractive to some highly qualified people as a fill-in while they look for a higher level business or professional position.

Targeting the People You Want

For most products and services, an ad which starts off with the word "Sales" will be fine. But for certain industries which attract people who want to sell in that specific field, an ad starting off with the name of that field will be a good draw, such as "Computer Sales."

The more you can target your ad to appeal to people interested in selling your particular product, rather than in sales generally, the better your ad will screen for you. You may get fewer calls, but those who do call are likely to be more interested.

However, to avoid missing people who don't see your more specialized ad, it is a good idea to place the more general type of sales ad also. Just be aware that you may get different types of callers from each ad, so that you can use the difference in results to help you decide the best approach when you're ready to advertise again.

When I used two ads for travel sales, the Sales-Travel ad pulled twice as many calls (around 60) as a second ad which said the same thing under the heading Travel-Sales. However, only a third of the Sales-Travel callers were interested in an interview, and only half showed up. Of these, only five people wanted to sell the program.

With the Travel-Sales ad, which was more closely targeted to the travel field, there were fewer callers, about 30. But half scheduled interviews, and almost all showed up. Of this group, 10 out of 15 wanted to sell the trips, and those who answered the Travel-Sales ad stayed with the company longer.

What to Say in Your Ad

Commonly, the larger companies have the big ads for sales people. But an ad of only a few lines can still get a good response, while keeping costs down. What's most important is to highlight the product or service the person will be selling and to indicate the main requirements, conditions, and rewards of the job. For example, our five-line travel ad that pulled so well said only:

Sales-Travel

> Sell trips to Kenya, Egypt, and China to groups and organizations part-time. Commission only, plus free trips possible. Dir. sales exper. preferred. Creative Travel. 555-2767.

In those five lines, we covered all of the basic questions: What is the person going to be selling? What method of selling will be used? Is it full time, part time, or does the person have an option? How is the person paid? Are there any special rewards, bonuses, perks of the job? What kind of qualifications are required? What kind of background does the person need?

Use a name. As a source to call about the ad, I suggest using either the name of a firm or a last name, plus the telephone number. Using the name of a specific person or company name is more inviting than a number alone. Also, a firm name or last name is more professional than using someone's first name, as in "Ask for Joe."

Another advantage of using a name is that it allows you to code your ads, so you'll know which one people are responding to. Just use a different name in each ad, and keep track of the calls under each name.

A tally is the simplest way to do this, and keeping track of who makes appointments in response to each ad allows you to measure the quality of responses as people show up for appointments, get involved, and are successful or unsuccessful in selling.

Specify times you are available. If there are only certain times when calls will be answered or a message phone is on, specify a time to call in your ad. Normally, people assume the ad means Monday through Friday from 9 to 5 unless the ad says otherwise, though you'll still get calls at other times.

It's best to set things up so callers can talk to someone right away about setting up a meeting if there is mutual interest. Otherwise, potentially good people may be lost to you if you are hard to reach.

HANDLING THE CALLS

Be ready with a prepared response when people call. You'll use one approach if the calls are answered live; another if you're using a phone message. In either case, a high percentage of the people who call are not going to be interested. They may say that they are but not call back to make an appointment or not show up.

Be prepared and view the recruiting process as a kind of funnel, much like the selling process. From your initial approach to the final sale (or the recruiting of a successful sales person) a decreasing percentage of those you first speak to will stay involved. When people don't follow through as promised, just cross them off your list.

You can take some steps to compensate for this, to be discussed later, such as setting up group interviews for several people, or arranging to use the time to do something else when someone doesn't show up for an interview.

Answering Calls Live

You should have a general outline or script to follow. You can identify yourself by the name in the ad, especially if you're using coded ads. When you actually meet people who come for interviews, you can always introduce yourself by your real name. In fact I have found with a small company that it's more impressive to give the idea that someone else has set up the interviews.

I suggest dividing your script or outline into major parts, and plan on your initial conversation taking no more than one or two minutes. Callers will want to know more about the job and the pay and you want to know about them.

If a caller has a lot of questions, simply explain that these will be answered during the interview and suggest setting up an appointment. Don't get into a long conversation. A person who's that interested should be willing to make an appointment to talk with you in person.

Call Answer Outline

The outline for handling calls should include an introductory statement setting up the call, a brief position description, questions about the caller, a response to the caller's questions, and a request for an interview.

Introductory statement. Explain what you will cover in the call: what the job is about, questions about the caller's background, and if there seems to be mutual interest, arrangements for an interview.

For instance, you might say, "Thanks for calling. I'd like to tell you a little about the job and then find out about your own background in sales for (name your industry). Then, if you're still interested and it seems like there's a fit, I'd like to set up an interview with you."

Brief position description. You can repeat what's already in the ad but elaborate a little. For example: "We represent a travel wholesaler and we're looking for someone to sell trips to our destinations, Kenya, Egypt, and China, to groups and organizations. It's a part-time commission position and we'll train."

A few questions about the caller. You want to see if the caller would be appropriate to sell for you. For instance, you might say, "Now, can you tell me a little about yourself? What background do you have in sales or travel?"

Listen to how callers speak on the phone and to what they say. Sales people should be well spoken and articulate. This is even more important than a background in sales or in your industry, because so much of selling involves talking to others on the phone. It's a good reason for screening out a caller who has trouble with it.

Comment favorably. If a caller has a favorable background, comment on this supportively. For example: "Well, good. It sounds like you might be really good for this position, since you've done all that. We've got a complete training program, but it helps when someone already has some good background experience."

If a caller's background is less relevant, but still promising and you offer training, say so, and encourage the person. For example: "Well, even if you don't have a sales background, it sounds like you'd be good at it, because you have done a lot of work with people before. Besides, as long as you're interested in learning, we can train you in what to do."

Turn down politely. If you feel that a caller isn't right for the position but hasn't already decided and told you so, simply explain politely why you feel the person wouldn't fit the position. Then say "thank you for calling," and "good bye." For example, "Well, we really are looking for someone with more experience in the field. But thanks so much for calling."

Respond to the caller's questions. Even if your description of the position is fairly complete, callers may still have questions. Be ready to answer a few if you can. It helps to prepare a list of anticipated questions and answers, so you can field questions.

This is much better than having people feel they have been talking to your answering service. Also it is better than having you end up calling back a lot of people who want answers before they will set up an appointment.

Limit your answers at this stage to two or three questions. If there are more, suggest that the rest be held until the interview, where they will be answered.

Set up an interview. If the caller is still interested after listening and sounds like a good person for the job, arrange an interview.

At this point, it's better to offer just one or two options for the time of the appointment. This suggests that there is competition for the position and that the interviewer has a busy schedule, making the position sound more impressive, important, and appealing.

If callers can't make an appointment they will tell you, and you can always offer to see if you can work around their schedules if other times are more convenient.

When you set up an interview, tell the caller if it's going to be one-on-one or a small group. Emphasize that it's important for people to call back if they can't make it, because the interviewer will be counting on them being there. This makes most people take the appointment more seriously, and encourages them to call if they change their minds. You still may get some no-shows, but not as many.

Finally, ask callers to give you their phone numbers, just in case. Then, if you need to reschedule, you can always call to make a change.

An example. A typical request to set up an interview might go something like this:

"So, if you'd like to discuss this further, we can set up an appointment for an interview. I've got some openings at three on Tuesday and four on Wednesday. How would those be for you?

"Good, let's set that up. Now, if something else should come up and you change your mind, would you please be sure to call? Otherwise, we'll be looking forward to seeing you then.

"Finally, I'd like to get your phone number, just in case we have to call you about something.

"Thanks, and we'll see you on (day and time of appointment you have just set up to confirm)."

Using a Recorded Message

A recorded telephone message should give callers additional information on the position by describing what they will be doing, how much they will be paid, and what kind of qualifications or background are preferred.

Start with a brief introduction to let callers know they have reached the right number and explain that the recording will tell more about the position. After you describe the position, responsibilities, payment, and qualifications, specify any specific benefits or bonuses and how much of a time commitment is involved. Finally, ask the prospect to call another number to schedule an interview if interested.

Here's a recording we used for people calling in response to the travel ad quoted earlier.

"Hello. You have reached Creative Travel. If you are calling about the sales position we have open, this message will give you additional details on the position. If you are interested, please call the number at the end of this message to arrange for an interview.

"We are looking for five or six sales people to market our trips around the San Francisco Bay area to companies and organizations.

"We represent a major national wholesaler based in New York who organizes trips to Kenya, Egypt, Greece, China, and Morocco. Your job will be to contact the representatives of these groups to set up trips for the whole group, so the earnings can be quite substantial. We will supply you with leads and you can develop your own.

"You can work on this part time, and there are sales management positions available. You will receive a commission on all sales, and it will also be possible to earn free trips as a bonus.

"We're looking for someone who has had previous direct sales experience or has enthusiasm and initiative and is willing to learn. We provide a complete training program.

"We've scheduled some times for some small group interviews on Tuesday, Wednesday, and Thursday afternoon. If you're still interested, please call (900) 555-2747 and ask for Ms. Randolph to set up an interview. Once again, that's (900) 555-2747."

Generally, those who call aren't likely to have many questions, since the most common ones have been answered in the recording. So setting up the interview is usually fairly routine.

10
Interviewing Sales People

Not everyone shows up for scheduled interviews. Some of them may have found other jobs, decided to do something else, or encountered some problem. In general, about half of the people who make appointments actually show up for group interviews, and about three-quarters for individual interviews.

INDIVIDUAL VERSUS GROUP INTERVIEWS

Should you use individual interviews, group interviews, or a combination of both? It depends. How many people you are hiring? How complex is your product or service is to explain? How many people do you have to talk to? How much time do you have?

For example, if you are seeking only one or two people, individual interviews make more sense. You will want to get a personal feel for each prospect, because you'll be working closely together. On the other hand, if you want to hire a group of people to handle different territories or types of contacts, use group interviews to select those you want to talk with further.

Complexity and Response Rate

The complexity of your presentation is important. If it's quick and simple, you have time to meet with prospects individually to explain everything. On the other hand, if you have to go into detail to show exactly what you're offering and how to sell it, then it's a good idea to use a group interview format in the preliminary stage.

For example, in marketing the travel program, we had video tapes about our trips, as well as some detailed information about our commission program and approach to groups and organizations. So it made sense to use the group format, rather than repeating the presentation in several one-on-one interviews.

Also look at the response rate. If you receive only a few replies, then individual interviews might be the way to go, barring other important considerations. On the other hand, if you're overwhelmed with callers, a group interview might be best.

A group interview will allow you to meet all those who passed your phone screening and still want to talk. In this way, you won't have to cut off potentially good prospects because of lack of time.

Weigh the following key factors in choosing the type of interview, according to what is most important to you.

	Factors Favoring	
Key Considerations	Individual Interviews	Group Interviews
Number of positions	One or two	Three or more
Complexity of explanation	Quick and simple	Long and involved
Number of responses	Few	Many

Whatever format you decide on, you can still be flexible as various circumstances arise. For example, if someone sounds enthusiastic and highly qualified but can't make it to a scheduled group meeting, perhaps you can meet with that person individually.

SETTING THE STAGE FOR THE INTERVIEW

As in many other situations today, impressions and images really count in an interview. Whether you're interviewing one person or several at a time, it's important to carefully set the stage to present prospects with an image of a successful, growing, and dynamic company.

If you have an attractive, impressive-looking office for individual interviews or access to a nice conference room for group interviews, that's ideal. But if you don't, you can rent an office or conference room on an hourly basis from companies which provide a full range of office and secretarial services. Some charge a monthly retainer for a minimal presence in the office, while others rent on an availability basis. It's an easy way to appear successful when you're first getting started or have limited funds. This image is important in persuading good sales people to represent you.

Sales Literature and Background Questionnaire

When people first arrive for the interview, have some of your promotional material available for them to look through. Also, this is a good time to give out a background information sheet or questionnaire for them to fill out. Later, during the individual interview, you can go over this with the applicant. In a group interview, you can hold on to these for review after the introductory presentation. These questionnaires will give you an idea of each person's background in sales, work preferences, and how much time is available to put into the project. In a group interview, a sign-up list is a good way to keep track of how many callers have shown up.

Checklist for the Interview

It's a good idea to use a checklist in preparing presentations, so you have the necessary materials to show or hand out to prospective sales people and any equipment you need. For example, when setting up a sales team in the travel field, we rented a conference room and set up materials so when people arrived they could pick up a background information questionnaire to fill out, along with various brochures on the company, the trips, and the marketing-commission plan. To be sure all of the slides, projectors, travel books, and presentation folders were on hand, we used the following checklist. You can adapt ours or create your own.

Equipment Needed
VCR
Monitor
Slide projector
Screen
Slide trays
Extension cords

Handouts and Introductory Information
Brochures
Flyers
Marketing or commission plan
Product information
Catalog sheets

Other Materials
Sign-up sheet
Background questionnaire
Marketing techniques book
Sales training tapes
Samples of sales aids
Video tape
Audio tape
Slides
Other (list)

In my experience, all of the extra time on advance preparation is well worthwhile. It helps to make interviews go smoothly. And it helps to impress prospects, making them likely to want to work for you.

Establish Rapport

As in meeting anyone new, you should start with a few minutes of conversation to build rapport. This helps the other person feel more comfortable and it helps you feel comfortable yourself. Use this as a chance to get to know a little about the other person and see if you have common interests.

One on one. In the one-on-one interview, start with small talk. Did the person find your office easily? Is the person busy with lots of interviews now? Or maybe make a few comments yourself about something, such as how much response you've been getting or how glad you are the person could make the interview at this time and get through the traffic without any problems. If you've had a chance to look at the person's questionnaire or resume, perhaps comment on something here that impresses you and then make a few more comments based on the person's response.

Group. In group interviews, I've found that asking people to introduce themselves helps. I set the tone by introducing myself briefly and then ask the others to give their names and say a few words about who they are, what they do, their experience in sales, if any, and why they answered the ad. This approach helps to make everyone feel at home and provides a little insight into each person. It gives you a sense of the person to whom you are talking, so that you can orient your presentation accordingly.

THE INTERVIEW

In the interview itself, present the sales opportunity in the best possible light and also carefully assess the prospect. Interviewing involves mutual screening. Just as you're deciding if you want someone in your sales group, that person is deciding whether to join.

You should start the interview on time. Even if only one or two people show up, wait no more than 5 or at most 10 minutes beyond the scheduled time, out of respect for the people who have come on time. Latecomers can always talk to you later about what they have missed.

For efficiency, it helps to divide the interview into three parts, much like the phone call. First, give a brief presentation about your product or service, showing what it is, why it's good, and how the sales person will benefit from selling it.

Second, gather information about the prospective sales person (or people in a group interview). Then, if you feel your prospect (or at least one in a group situation) is a likely recruit, you can go into more detail on your program and expectations. If not, you can end the interview.

Presenting Your Product or Service

Consider the first part of the interview as your own sales presentation. You want to show prospective sales people why they should market your product or service. Not only are you selling that, but you're selling them on the advantages of working for you. To do this, you must answer several key questions your prospective sales people will have in mind:

What am I going to be selling?
What are its benefits?
How does it compare with the competition?
What are the credentials of the company?
How am I going to be selling it: phone, personal contact, referral?
To whom am I going to sell it: individuals, groups, companies?
What kind of sales materials will I have?
How much am I going to make by selling it?
How am I going to be paid?
What kind of leads, training, and coordination will you provide?

The presentation stage of the interview should be designed to provide answers quickly (in 5 to 10 minutes) to these questions. This is where sales and training materials discussed earlier become important.

They show that you have the back-up materials and support for your sales people. If you are using a one-on-one interview format, you can cover these questions informally. In a group situation, plan on a more structured and formal presentation.

Information on your product or service and the company. This is the time to show your product or service and any literature you have developed which describes it. If your product needs to be demonstrated, such as a mechanical device or book on time planning, do that. If you have brochures, catalog sheets, or a background sheet on the company, give them out. If you have promotional clips or testimonials about your product or company, show these too.

One approach is to hand out product, company and promotional materials to people as they come to the interview. Alternatively, these materials can be included in a presentation folder for people to look at. As people are looking at this material or after they have reviewed it, briefly talk about your product or service, making sure to cover the following points: major benefits, how it compares to the competition and where it is better, track record of the product or service to date, and the company's credentials. You're selling your company and your product or service to prospective sales people. They need to feel both are saleable in order to get behind you.

Sales approach to be used. Identify the target market and tell how you envision your sales people reaching it. If your audience is already experienced in sales techniques, you may not need to go into much detail here, since they will already know what to do. But otherwise, explain some of your sales ideas so the sales people will understand and feel comfortable with what they have to do.

For example, some people don't mind calling prospective customers on the phone. They've done plenty of phoning before. But if they have to make a personal presentation, they may not know how to do it. Alternatively, others hate cold calling on the phone, but love meeting people in person. Decide on the best approach for you. Will one person have to do both? Can they choose their own techniques? Can you coordinate people with complementary skills to work as a team?

Explain briefly what they have to do and show them any additional sales materials they will be using, such as telephone sales scripts or presentation books.

This section of your presentation should cover these major points in a sentence or two:

Target market for the product (age, income level, lifestyle).

Types of groups or individuals to contact (associations, companies, non-profit organizations, individuals).

How to contact these groups (cold calling, personal presentations, referrals).

Where leads will come from (from you, the sales person's own initiative, or both).

Sales materials available (catalog sheets, price lists, scripts, presentation books).

Source of materials (Are you supplying the materials at no cost? Do sales people have to make their own copies? Is there a charge for sales materials?).

By going over these issues, you show prospective sales people that you have thought through the sales techniques for selling your product or service. This helps them feel confident that they can do it also.

Payment arrangements. Now comes the real meat and potatoes, "What's in it for me?" Describe your compensation plan, and show how it translates into hourly, weekly, or monthly earnings.

This is the time to hand out copies of your plan, so your prospects can see, in black and white, what's possible. Briefly explain how the plan works, and possibly use a flip chart, poster, or blackboard to help. The kinds of points to cover here include:

What is the base commission (and draw if any)?

What are the earnings on an average sale?

How many sales are likely on a day? In a week? About how many sales can be made in an hour? Or for a more expensive product, how many hours are typical for a sale?

How do these typical sale patterns work into average earnings per hour? For 10/20/30/40 hours a week?

What kind of bonuses are possible for good sales?

Are there overrides for supervising or recruiting other sales people? If so, go into the structure of your sales network, using a chart.

What sort of track record, if any, do other sales people have who have worked with you or others in the company? If there's no track record because it's a new company or new way of selling the product or service, what makes you think sales will reach the level you project?

When or how frequently will people get paid?

You don't have to go into this information in great detail. In fact, you might just cover the highlights and wait until you have found out more about your prospects before you explain more. The point is to explain just enough so your interviewees feel working for you will be financially worth their while. You can go over detailed specifics later.

Training and support. Few sales people can simply go out and sell on their own for an extended time. They need to receive continuous direction, motivation, and support. Now's the time to show the kind of back-up you will provide.

For example, if you have worked up sample phone scripts, letters, and price comparisons and have not shown them yet, show them now. If you will be putting together updates and newsletters, publicity releases, or ads, use examples to illustrate.

If you plan a training program, such as using sales and motivational tapes in your meetings, explain that. And if you've worked out guidelines for selling or have a marketing training manual or other support you are providing, show them. Perhaps include them in a book you can flip through in your presentation.

The key types of support your prospects will want include:

Guidance on how to sell (such as sample phone scripts and letters).

Promotional materials for your product or service (such as publicity releases and ads).

Data to keep your sales people well informed on the market generally (such as sample price comparisons and surveys of the competition).

Creative marketing ideas.

Coordination in providing leads and preventing conflicts due to overlapping sales efforts.

Company image back-up, such as letterheads and business cards.

Day-to-day support you provide in the form of the use of an office, typewriter, phones, etc.

Training you offer through written materials and training meetings.

Regular meetings planned to provide motivation, guidance, and general coordination.

Obviously, you don't want to spend a great deal of time on the particulars of all the support materials, meetings, and training techniques you offer. The main thing is to show that all this support is available, so you can impress your prospects with how you can help them.

To a great extent, you can cover the range of help you offer by simply flipping through a presentation book and showing examples of phone scripts, letters, PR releases, ads, price comparisons, marketing idea lists, letterheads, and the like. Also, briefly list other types of support you offer, such as meetings, training aids, and office availability.

Getting Information and Assessing Your Prospects

Once you've completed a brief introduction you can swing into the second phase of the interview, finding out about your prospective sales people and assessing whether you would like them to work with you. Use the questionnaire, personal questions, and your own observations to assess these five main characteristics.

Appearance. Prospects should look neat and be well dressed and groomed. That's basic. Beyond that, consider the image you want for your company. In a company with a consumer product with broad appeal, perhaps anyone who looks businesslike and professional would be suitable. But in companies with a special product line a special look might be required, such as maturity and authority in selling to high-level executives or a sophisticated image to sell a beauty product line for career women.

General Attitude. The attitude you are looking for is one associated with success in sales. You will notice some of the right or wrong qualities as people talk and express themselves. For instance, you pick up right away a very optimistic, people-oriented approach by noticing friendliness and upbeat comments.

To find out about other qualities, such as willingness to persist, work hard, and be well organized, you may have to ask questions, such as "How many hours a week do you usually work?" or "Would you say you like detail work or not?"

Qualities of a good sales person
Positive attitude toward life.
Willingness to work hard.
Persistence.
Organization.
Attention to details.
Outgoing personality, likes people.
Enjoyment of competition.
Acceptance of challenges.
Willingness to take risks.
Strong desire to get ahead.

General Skills. Certain skills are associated with success in sales. Again, you can pick up some of these by observation or just by asking.

Good sales people are able to express themselves articulately and are willing to listen. The key to finding out what others want is listening; a sales person who talks too much, even if very well, can easily lose a sale by saying the wrong things.

Good sales people are also willing to learn and be taught, to take direction from you. They are interested in personal improvement. They are good with people; they can work well with both customers and the other members of your team.

Sales experience versus potential. You have to decide how much sales background you require and how much you're willing to train. People with enthusiasm, interest, and sales skills have excellent potential. If you're willing to spend the time training, consider them.

On the other hand, usually the more sales background a person has, particularly in your field, the better, because that person will be be productive sooner. If you decide to stick with experienced people, look for the following to assess experience:

Years of sales experience, including phone sales, personal presentations, and experience in your particular field (less important than having sales experience generally).

Track record of success in selling, as measured by previous earnings and any awards for good selling.

References and recommendations.

Participation in sales and business groups (suggests a strong commitment to sales).

Good fit with your team and approach. How well will the new people fit in with the rest of your team and how well can you work with them? To a great extent, this depends on how your organization is set up. For example, if you are recruiting many people who will be working fairly independently, this question may not be very pressing. If you plan to work closely with a small group, it matters a lot.

Assuming a good fit is important, the kinds of factors to look at include:

1. The geographic area where the person wants to work. This is important if you plan to assign territories, since you'll want to choose people for your team in different areas. You may need to choose between two people who want the same place; or perhaps one of them can be persuaded to work in a different spot.

2. The types of groups or organizations the person wants to contact. You need to know this information if you want people to specialize within the same area. If a person has strong contacts in a certain market segment you want to reach, this can be a key person to have on your team.

3. Special skills the person may have which can complement your sales program. For instance, people who have experience in giving talks and presentations might be tapped to benefit the whole group.

4. Amount of time available. Do people want to work part time? Full time? And if part time, do they have enough hours to make the kind of commitment you need for your program? For example, they should be willing to spend at least 5 to 10 hours a week if part time, and either meet with you and attend a meeting at least every two weeks or more.

5. Personality. Ask yourself, do you like this person? Do you feel comfortable? Do you feel the prospect will make a good team player with the mix of people you want on your team? Trust your gut feelings or intuitions. If you feel hesitant or feel mistrustful, you shouldn't work with this person.

Deciding Who to Recruit

Sometimes, by the end of the interview, you can make a recruiting decision and the prospective sales person can, too. It's preferable to come to this decision on the spot if you can, while the prospect is there and has just heard your presentation.

But if necessary, allow time to think it over. A prospect may be going for other interviews and need a chance to decide. Or maybe a prospect wants to review commitments for the next few weeks to be sure he or she has the time to commit to your company. In making a choice between two people for a certain territory you may want to talk to each person individually first.

Group interview. In a group situation, I recommend quickly glancing over the questionnaires when they are first turned in at the group meeting, before you start your presentation to the group. Then observe and listen carefully to get a general impression of each person's appearance, attitude, skill level, sales background or potential, and personality.

You will normally want to wait until after the meeting to talk one-on-one with those people who are still interested and who seem possible candidates. You can do this right after the group interview with those who want to stay around, or you can set up appointments for later.

One on one. In the one-on-one interview, you can usually get the information you want in the course of talking with a person, reviewing the questionnaire, and perhaps looking at a resume. If you decide you want the person, you can let him or her know right then.

If the interest is mutual, you can go on with the next phase of the interview, going into your program in more detail and explaining the logistics of coming aboard. If either you or the prospect decides against hiring, you can simply conclude the interview. If you or the prospect is unsure, go on with the interview and make your decision later.

Once you feel you would like to work with someone and the feeling seems mutual, here are some things you can do to familarize your prospect further with your operation.

Provide more complete details on your products or services and their market. Use a tape, video, or demonstration to help explain.

Provide additional information on the marketing approach being used and the commission you are paying. If you have prepared marketing materials or a booklet of techniques, give this out and discuss it.

Describe the back-up support you will provide now and in the next few weeks, such as distributing leads and having regular meetings.

Restate any requirements or expectations which you have for those joining your group, and ask for a commitment from those who come aboard (for example, an agreement to participate for at least 5 to 10 hours a week and to attend one weekly sales meeting).

Let people know what they need to do next (such as attend an orientation meeting to prepare them to sell your product or service or go out on a sales call with you).

Ask those who are interested to fill out your background questionnaire, if they haven't already done so.

Getting Off to a Quick Start

Once you decide to hire someone, have the next step already planned, so you can immediately involve the person in your sales effort. There are three major ways to do this. Invite a person who is ready to go right out and sell. Have the person accompany you or an experienced person on a sales call. Invite the person to attend an orientation program to go over the job in more detail and discuss how to sell.

Start them selling right away. Experienced sales people may feel ready to go out and begin selling. If you have a relatively simple program and they have a good sales background, this approach will probably work. In this case, you should encourage them to go out while their level of excitement is still high. Let them know you are open to other possibilities, such as having them join you on a sales call or attending an orientation. And invite them to call if they have any questions. Otherwise, if they want to sell right away and you feel confident they can do it, by all means let them.

Invite them with you on a sales call. This approach works especially well when you are recruiting just one or two new people and have the time to work with them personally. You show them what to do by having them watch you do it. They can listen in when you're making calls or go along to watch you make a presentation. Afterward you can discuss what happened. Perhaps they can do the next call or presentation while you observe, until they feel comfortable going out on their own.

This is a good approach to use after you've got a sales team organized and are adding recruits. New sales people can team up with experienced people. In this case, it is a good idea to have an override system in place in which the experienced sales person is sponsoring or supervising the newcomer in return for a bonus on that person's sales.

Give them an orientation. Conducting an orientation works best when you've recruited a number of new sales people at the same time. At the orientation, you can describe your product or service at length and explain some techniques new people can use to get out and sell. After this orientation, you can always offer individual help to people who want it.

11
Orienting New Sales People

Once you've decided to bring a new sales person aboard, the next step is helping that person get ready to sell. This keeps the momentum going, and avoids your new recruit losing interest while you get organized. As soon as sales people are recruited it is important to get them involved.

Start with an individual or group orientation, or one-on-one field demonstration, and discuss your program and how to sell it. Then, depending on circumstances and the new people's experience, you can do more training, either separately or in conjunction with sales meetings.

WHAT TO INCLUDE IN THE ORIENTATION

The main point in the orientation is to go into your product or service in detail, stressing the main selling points and techniques, so the new person feels ready to start selling. Whatever orientation approach you use, be sure to include the following elements.

Detailed Presentation of the Product or Service

Make a complete, detailed presentation of your product or service, to build product knowledge and confidence. Your sales people should fully understand what you do. Also, they should feel fully confident that the product or service is good, so they can share this conviction with others.

Make it a point to underline the product's or service's main benefits and important features and to emphasize how the product or service compares to the competition. If you have multiple products or services, go over the program as a whole and then deal with each product or service individually.

If you have a product line, go over the various items in the line, and explain how they are used and by whom. For example, if it's a jewelry line, show the various pieces, and describe the typical customer (such as a woman in her 30s or 40s from a middle-income household).

If it's a service, discuss the various categories of services offered (such as bookkeeping, payroll, preparation of financial statements) and who is the usual buyer (large corporations, small businesses, or doctors and professionals). Outline the prices for various services.

Review of Sales Materials

Show the presentation materials you have created for the customer or client. Go over any catalog sheets, flyers, brochures, testimonials, price lists, video tapes, presentation books, publicity handouts, or other materials which sales people will use in showing your product or service to the customer. Go over the contents, and how and when to use them.

If you have masters the sales people can use to make their own copies, hand them out and suggest ways to use them. For example, print on colored paper and add your name and phone number.

If you recommend putting together a presentation book, give examples of how you have done this and how to sit down with a customer and flip through the book.

If you've got demonstration material on videotape, show it and comment on how it can be used. If the tape runs more than ten minutes, invite the sales people to come back to view the tape.

Approaches to Closing the Sale

Review various ways to approach the customer and close the sale. How much to explain depends on how experienced your new sales people are. At least you should go over your specific policies and guidelines for selling, based on your own experience. For instance, if your sales people will be calling on corporate buyers, and you have found that companies in certain industries are more likely to buy, pass this on. If you have found that a certain sales technique works well for your product, describe and recommend this technique.

If you have printed guidelines and policies, this is the time to hand them out, going over the highlights to underline their importance. Point out that you are willing to be flexible and that your sales people should feel free to make suggestions for changes or to adapt your general approach to their own styles, as long as they follow your policies.

Plans for Future Meetings and Training

Lay out your schedule of meetings and training sessions, and make it clear what you expect by way of attendance and participation. For example, I believe it is important to have at least weekly or biweekly meetings to keep sales people involved and motivated. These meetings can be in either a group setting or individually with you.

I have found that those people who come to meetings are more likely to stay involved and committed. Without regular meetings, sales people working alone and on commission may lose their connection with you and drift away.

If you are planning to set up a training program, explain what you have in mind. For instance, explain if you will lead it yourself, use sales tapes, or bring in speakers. Ask your new sales people what they need at this point, so you can incorporate this into the training.

Don't spend much time on specific sales techniques if people already know them. On the other hand, don't leave out anything valuable. By combining your own ideas with those of your new people, you can supplement whatever they are doing on their own to improve their selling.

Sales Commission and Bonus Program

This part of the orientation should cover in depth exactly how your payment plan works. If you have a written policy sheet or marketing plan, take some time to review it, so you and your sales people know that everything is clear. You may want to use a flip chart or blackboard to help you explain.

Even if you covered compensation in your recruiting meeting, now is the time to review these arrangements in detail. Also use this discussion as an opportunity to motivate your team with incentives by emphasizing the benefits of good performance.

Specifically, highlight these points:

Basic commission and bonuses for high volume.
Overrides, if any, for sponsoring and supervising other sales people.
How the commission translates into money based on a typical sale.
How much money is likely to be earned in a day based on the
    number of likely sales per day.
How the commission rate translates into an hourly income.

By going into this payment program in depth, your sales people can gain a good idea of the likely return, which will help them decide how much time to commit to the program. In cases where it takes time to realize a commission from a sale, make this very clear, so sales people can plan ahead.

For instance, in some fields, there may be a high commission on a single sale, but it may take several months before the sale is finalized and the money earned, as in selling real estate or in the travel business, where sales people aren't usually paid until customers use their tickets and return successfully from a trip.

Point out any procedural arrangements, such as what must be done to get credit for a sale, such as putting a code number on an application, filling out a form, or providing a referral name for credit if the prospect becomes a buyer.

Finally, if you have several sales people who may experience some overlap in the same area, go over how multiple contacts will be handled. For example, you may prefer to split the commission based on each person's contribution, or perhaps give credit to the person who actually closes the sale.

Sales Aids and Training Materials

Go over the sales aids and training materials the sales people will be using initially, briefly highlighting any other materials you give them to review for future use. Focus on what they should do to get started right away, so that they aren't confused by too many ideas or too much information.

For instance, if you have a phone script and follow-up letters, give them out and briefly explain how they should be used. If you have a list of steps to get started, go over them so that each sales person has an immediate plan of action. If you have a leads list, pass it out, and suggest step-by-step guidelines for developing new leads.

Other sales aids you may want to give out at this time include sample price lists, sample ads, a list of marketing ideas, and a list of recommended resource materials.

Letterhead Stationery and Business Cards

Some companies start by giving sales people their own personal business cards right away. Others wait a short time until it seems likely that the new people will work out.

In either case, you can give out business cards with only the company name, address and number, and you can provide letterhead stationery (or give out a master, so people can make their own).

Other Handouts

Finally, if you have a newsletter or provide updates, give them out, at least the current issues and possibly some back issues, to let new sales people know what you have been doing.

If you have several sales people and it's appropriate for them to work together, hand out a list of your current sales group or associates. If you have an experienced sales person, team her or him with a newcomer and work out a commission split accordingly. However, the decision to work together should come from your people. Use your list to suggest combinations, but leave it up to them to choose.

I have found it helpful to give out these lists right away, since I have had many inexperienced people who wanted to team up with others. However, it may be wise to wait until you feel confident your new people are going to stay with you. Otherwise, a person who drops out may use your list to recruit your people to something else. Use your own judgement in deciding what's best.

INDIVIDUAL ORIENTATION

An individual orientation makes the most sense when you are recruiting only one or two new people. It gives you time to talk with each person independently. It also works well when you have a strong sales group with an override system, where you can assign new sales people to others for orientation and supervision.

Combine with a Demonstration

An ideal way to use an individual orientation is in combination with a field demonstration, taking a new person with you on a sales call or showing what you do on the phone. Depending on your style, you can do this in several ways: Do the demonstration first, then follow with a discussion about what happened and what the person should do. Combine the demonstration with an orientation. Or go through a more detailed introduction and then take the recruit out on a sales call. If a person is experienced and has received a comprehensive orientation, a demonstration may not be necessary.

Tailor to Fit

In the course of the orientation, you should cover the topics previously mentioned. However, since you're talking one to one, you can cover these topics informally, and personalize your presentation to suit the needs of the new people.

For example, suppose a sales person is interested in targeting a certain market because it feels more comfortable, such as a woman teacher doing part-time sales who wants to contact educational organizations and schools. Emphasize those aspects of your product line or service which will appeal most to that group.

Or suppose a person feels more comfortable with a sales approach that doesn't involve telephoning. Show that person how to start right away using only non-phone techniques, such as talking to program chairmen at meetings, sending out letters, or passing out flyers and brochures at organizational events.

Build Rapport

Use the individual orientation to get to know your new sales people, as well as to detail the product or sales information they need to know. This personal touch is a way to build rapport, which is an important part of motivation.

Equally important is each person's desire to feel competent, powerful, productive, and appreciated. Your support can help your people feel this way.

GROUP ORIENTATION

The group orientation format is ideal when you're bringing in a group of sales people to market a program, or expect only some of the new people to stay with the program. A group orientation can serve a number of purposes besides simply getting people ready to sell.

First, it can help to create a team spirit, a feeling of working together. Second, it can help you find out where sales people are most interested in working, so you can provisionally divide up your territories. Third, you can use the orientation for additional screening to see who is really serious about working with you.

I found the following approach worked well when I was organizing a sales group, and I recommend it to others.

Set up Meetings at the First Interviews

Invite the people from your initial interviews who express interest to attend a group orientation. Work out preferred meeting times, and set up one or two orientation meetings for three to eight people each.

I scheduled one meeting in the morning for people with days available, and one in the evening for people who already had full-time jobs. Follow up to let people know when the meetings are.

Keep a List of Promised Attendees

Make a list of the people you expect to come, and unless someone has a good excuse, eliminate no-shows from your sales team. You'll find those who are casual about attending this first meeting are likely to be casual about marketing your product or service.

Organize Your Handouts

Decide on the materials you plan to hand out in advance, and lay them out so that people can easily get a complete set. I organized the materials I planned to hand out (marketing plan, flyers, brochures, marketing techniques manual, sample phone scripts and letters, etc.) into piles on a table. As people arrived, I invited everyone to take a set of materials, explaining that we would be going over them.

At the end of the meeting, you can pass out letterhead stationery and business cards to those who are still serious about marketing the program.

Use a Meeting Agenda

Make up an agenda listing the topics you want to cover in order of presentation. I personally like the sequence outlined at the beginning of this chapter, but feel free to adapt the format to your own style.

If anyone is late, wait no more than 5 to 10 minutes before beginning, to show respect for the people who came on time, and fill in latecomers after the meeting.

Go over the major topics listed in your agenda, and ask people to ask questions, if they have any, after you finish each topic or at the end of your formal presentation. In my meetings, I covered the major topics, referred people to the handouts as appropriate, and then asked for questions.

Begin with Introductions and Background

Start with introductions to help everyone feel at home and find out about the people in your group. Say who you are, describe your plans for the company, and ask people to introduce themselves briefly.

I found that this helped everyone feel comfortable with one another and also gave me a sense of who people were and where they might work well in marketing the program.

In particular, I asked people to describe their backgrounds in sales and in the field generally, to indicate where they were from, and to state how involved they wanted to be in selling the program (under 10 hours a week, 10 to 20, or more).

If you don't already have background questionnaires, ask people to fill these out now, and also indicate when and in what part of the sales territory they would like to work.

Make Office Arrangements

I made arrangements for those who wished to use the office to make phone calls and send out letters. If your office is available for your sales people to use, work out the appropriate arrangements. For example, find out who wants to work at home, and who wants to use the office. If you need to, schedule times when different people can use the office, and ask people to sign up to use it.

Set Up Training Sessions

I arranged attendance for an ongoing series of sales and training meetings each week. Work out arrangements for the best time to conduct these meetings and training sessions.

Find out, based on peoples' past sales experience, who is interested in an ongoing training program, and schedule that if appropriate. A good time to do this might be for 30 minutes to an hour before or after the regular meeting. Then those who want to can come for the training as well as the meeting.

Schedule Sales Meetings

Get a sense of how often people are willing to come to sales meetings. Once a week is ideal, but if that turns out to be tough for a number of people, perhaps schedule a meeting every two weeks. This is the minimum, in my opinion, for keeping a sales group together.

Decide on the best time or times for the most people, and schedule the meeting now. Preferably, have just one meeting.

If it's difficult to get everyone together, which it may be with people working part-time, then schedule one in the morning or afternoon for the people who are free days and would prefer to do their sales work during the day, and one in the evening for those who work days and are free at night.

Review and Wrap Up

If people feel ready, and you agree, let them know that they can start selling the program right away. Review the steps they can use for immediate sales.

If people don't feel ready, or simply want additional selling tips, indicate that you will be glad to work with them individually or in a group to provide further training. Suggest a follow-up training meeting or invite people to join you for a field demonstration of your own sales techniques.

Indicate that you're always receptive to further questions and want to do all you can to help your people be successful. Welcome their feedback and comments, too. Then end the meeting.

At this point, everyone should have a plan for how they will proceed and be ready to go.

FIELD DEMONSTRATIONS

Used with either an individual or group orientation, a one-on-one field demonstration is an excellent orientation and training tool. You can do it yourself or have an experienced person in your sales group do it. It is an ideal approach if you are using an override or sponsorship system, where new recruits are typically brought in under an experienced person.

The demonstration works well for both phone calls and regular sales presentations. It gives the new recruit a first-hand look at selling by people who know how.

Then, after some observation, new people can try to make a sale themselves while the experienced person looks on. It is also a good idea to discuss what to watch for, what happened, and how the presentation worked out.

Demonstrating Telephone Selling

To illustrate the phone approach, I invited new people recruited to market a savings club program to listen in on an extension when I made a series of initial cold calls to potential customers. Then I gave out a rough script to use as a guideline and asked them to try a few calls on their own while I listened in.

Afterward, we talked about how I did what I did and why. I asked them how they felt about what they did. I made some suggestions, and asked them for their ideas on doing better next time.

Demonstrating the Personal Sales Call

Here is an example of a typical sales-call demonstration. I went on a call with a salesman for a collection agency service, which normally uses the hands-on approach to train new sales people. I observed while the salesman called to confirm his appointment. As we drove to the first stop, a hotel where he hoped to persuade the bookkeeper to turn over all her collection accounts to the agency, he explained what he was going to do.

First, he planned to make a little small talk to establish rapport. Then he would swing into his presentation, emphasizing why the hotel needed this service, and how much time and money it would save.

He showed me a book of details on the services offered, along with some testimonial letters about the company. He also described some of the sales techniques he would be using to establish rapport, such as repeating the bookkeeper's name frequently as he talked. Thus I had a complete picture of what to expect before we arrived at the meeting.

When we went in, he introduced me as his assistant, and then went into his presentation. Since he had already prepped me on what to look for, I was especially aware of the sales methods he was using: the small talk opening, some questions to learn about the hotel's collection problems and needs, the brief highlighting of benefits, a detailed discussion of programs the agency offered and how they could be tailored to the hotel's needs, and finally some questions leading to the close.

Afterward, when we stopped for coffee, we went over in detail exactly what he had done, so I could better understand how to use the techniques myself.

Key Points to Follow

Some of the major points to keep in mind for field-demonstration training are as follows.

Spend some time before the demonstration discussing what you are going to do. Alert the new sales person on what to look for and what role to play, such as your assistant taking notes. Note the phases of your presentation, the sales materials you will be using, and the sales methods you will employ.

To help the new person recall what you've done, provide a script or agenda as a guide.

Let the client or customer know what role the new sales person has (your assistant taking notes, for example). This way, the customer won't be sitting there thinking about unanswered questions while you're trying to focus attention on your sales presentation.

Do the demonstration exactly as you would with an ordinary sales call.

Afterward, review what you have done, and highlight the sales techniques which have been particularly effective.

This is also a good time to ask the new sales person for observations, reactions and opinion on how the presentation can be improved.

Demonstration Selling

Field demonstration training is especially useful for a sales person who will use a demonstration to sell a product or service, such as a cooking demonstration to sell pots, a facial demonstration to sell beauty products, or a tasting event to try out food. The sales people can see for themselves, in dramatic form, exactly how the selling is done.

As an alternative, some companies use a videotape of a hands-on demonstration, but there's more impact when new sales people go out into the field themselves. The conversation before and after the demonstration also helps focus attention on some of the key techniques being used.

In some cases, after the initial demonstration and discussion, new sales people feel ready to sell. But often, especially with inexperienced people, it takes a few demonstrations to create confidence. And those products or services that are relatively complex to sell require several demonstrations.

Practice Makes Perfect

It is a good idea gradually to involve new people by having them handle one part of the presentation. For example, the experienced person can handle the opening, close, and the more important parts of the demonstration, such as a discussing the major benefits and answering objections.

The trainee can demonstrate or describe some of the detail. Once trainees are comfortable doing that, they can do a little more each time, until they are ready to go out on their own.

When to Put Them on Their Own

Some companies, after this first demonstration stage, let new sales people work on their own. In others, sales mangers who want more control go along to observe new sales people and give feedback, until they both feel the sales person is ready to work independently. Or a new person may volunteer to team up with a more experienced sales person for a while.

Conclusions

There are lots of options to field demonstrations. It depends in part on your personal style, how involved it is to sell your product or service, and the background of your new sales people. Even experienced sales people may want to observe a demonstration when they are going to represent a new company.

In general, the demonstration approach is an excellent way of getting new people, whether experienced or not, introduced to selling your product or service. It's a way to get people out into the field and selling right away.

12
Organizing Effective Sales Meetings

Once new sales people are oriented and committed to join your company, it is important to have regular sales meetings. Even if you have only one or two people working with you, plan a regular time to meet. And at least have a long conversation by phone with people working in distant areas.

Schedule meetings or calls once a week, at a minimum every two weeks. Make it clear that you and they need to stay in touch at least this often. Otherwise, you will find that people drift away, and once they do it is hard to get them back to their initial enthusiasm and commitment.

PLANNING SALES MEETINGS

In planning your meetings, recognize that sales meetings have a number of key functions. At times, there will be more focus on one function than on another, but all play their part in keeping people involved and motivated.

The overall purposes of a sales meeting include social networking, giving out information, getting feedback, planning, coordination, organization, developing sales strategies, sales training, motivation and inspiration, recognition, and planning the next meeting.

Social Networking

An important part of every meeting is the social interaction that goes on among the members of your sales group, as well as between them and you. Such networking helps to create social ties that bind people together and to your organization. It also helps make working as part of the team enjoyable, making people feel more motivated and committed to company goals. Naturally, it's important to have a good balance between socializing and work; otherwise, with too much socializing, people can become distracted from work.

Thus, you should allow some time at the beginning or end of your meeting for people to get together. Perhaps offer coffee or snacks or combine the meeting with a meal to encourage socializing. But then, after the social networking period is over, get down to business, and make it clear that it's time to focus on the central purpose of the meeting.

New Company and Product Information

The meeting is an ideal time to make new product announcements and hand out new product materials, such as catalog sheets or flyers. Likewise, you can provide updates on anything happening with the company. In making these announcements, be sure to go over product highlights and benefits, and comment on what's most important about the materials you hand out. Otherwise, they may often go unread.

Besides providing the latest information on your company and product, a sales meeting also can be used for sharing general information in the field or opinions on recent world events and how they are likely to affect your business. For instance, there may be a change in the law that will affect your packaging. Competitors may have introduced competing products your people should know about. There may be upcoming consumer or trade shows in your industry that your sales people would like to attend.

Promotional Ideas and Plans

If you are sending out any publicity or advertising, this is a good place to describe what you have in mind and get feedback. You may find the people in your group have some good suggestions, and you want to be sure they are behind any promotion you are planning. If they know what publicity or advertising is likely to be used, they can plan for it, and perhaps use this material to back them up in a presentation.

By the same token, as articles or ads about your product or service appear, let your sales group know. If something about you or your company appears in the mass media, it suggests that you are doing something right.

Product or Service Demonstrations

Demonstrations are ideal when you add new products or services. You can also use demonstrations to show good sales techniques. Such demonstrations can range anywhere from hands-on demonstrations of equipment and taste tests of food products, to videotape presentations of people enthusiastically using your product.

Reports and Feedback From the Field

You will find meetings are an excellent time to find out what everyone is doing. In some organizations, only the person at the top really knows what everyone is doing, since each individual is guided by the head person. However, I feel people work better together if everyone has a sense of what is happening throughout the organization. This gives them a baseline for comparing themselves to others and staying motivated through group team spirit in achieving a common goal. Then, too, having such open feedback creates a generally open, supportive context, in which people feel more attuned to helping and supporting one another.

Sharing sales information. Another advantage of getting reports and feedback in a group is that people can use the information from others to improve their own sales efforts in the field. Conversely, if someone has encountered a problem, that person can get ideas from others who may have had a similar experience in the field. Even if they haven't had the same experience, they still might have some good ideas. Additionally, you can use feedback to find out not only what works, but what doesn't. Then you can use this information for collective problem solving.

Identifying needs. Does anybody want anything from you? More product materials? More samples? More master flyers? More scripts or guidelines for phone calls? This is the time to find out exactly what people want, so you can provide it, by the next meeting or before.

Planning

Meetings are an opportunity to plan where you are going both for the short and long term. The possibilities are endless. At these meetings you can decide what you want to do, determine who is going to carry out various roles, and work out a schedule of tasks. It is especially valuable to use meetings for planning because you involve members of your sales group, giving them the feeling of participation in planning.

Daily logistics. An important planning function of meetings is working out the details of what everyone is going to be doing over the next few days. For example, if people need to make arrangements for using the office or phones at certain times, schedule this. If you need to find out who people are contacting to avoid overlapping contacts, ask for this information so you can coordinate the process. You can also use meetings for distributing leads, although this can be handled on a one-on-one basis, too.

Group activities and events. Besides the overall planning and coordination of what everyone is doing individually, meetings are ideal for planning and coordinating activities and events you want to do as a group. Some typical examples are

Working out arrangements to attend a trade show.
Doing a mass distribution of leaflets at an event.
Putting on a cold-calling campaign in a downtown area, where each
     person covers different floors in a building.
Attending an industry conference or exhibit together.
Creating a social occasion such as a picnic or potluck supper.

Sales Strategies and Training

This is a good time for making recommendations on selling certain products or contacting certain target markets. Your people will have ideas, too. With experienced sales people, you can spend less time on this, but with new people, this discussion is especially important to help them know exactly what to do.

For example, many new sales people frequently don't know how to find their own leads, so you might devote a strategy discussion to that. Or perhaps you can pass out a list of suggested places to go and people to contact.

Sales training can be a regular part of every meeting, or optional for those who are interested. Discussion or demonstration of different sales techniques will help people expand their own repertoires of sales skills. This is a little different from suggesting specific sales approaches.

After a session on general skills, its a good idea to talk about how these skills might be applied to selling your particular product or service. Either make suggestions yourself or invite people in your group to discuss how they would do it.

If you're good in sales training, you can lead this part of the meeting yourself. Or you might find it helpful to use tapes or videos made by experienced sales trainers. For example, in our meetings we listened to such tapes for about 20 minutes, then discussed how to use the technique just covered to increase our own sales.

Motivation and Recognition

Just having a sales meeting can be a source of motivation and inspiration to the people who attend. However, you can also incorporate activities which are specifically designed to motivate and inspire.

For example, allow some time for people to share their accomplishments. This is a great way to get people fired up, because they have been recognized for their achievements—or they see what someone else has done, which may trigger a competitive spark.

Another possibility is to have a guest speaker who comes with a motivational message. Still other groups listen to a brief motivational tape or read inspirational messages about success.

Besides having people share accomplishments, you can do other things at meetings to recognize and reward people, thereby encouraging everybody to greater efforts. For instance, set aside time at monthly meetings to give out certificates of achievement, ribbons, trophies, or plaques.

Maybe use special gifts, such as pendants, rings, or motivational books. Or have an extra monetary bonus as a reward. You might also consider having special titles for your awards, such as "Best Salesperson of the Month," "Highest Volume Producer," or "Most New Accounts of the Month."

Some sales leaders turn these recognition meetings into gala occasions themselves, and combine them with a picnic, party, rally, or other special event. Obviously, the larger your sales group, the more you can do to make recognition a big thing. Even with a few people, you can show your appreciation with a token gift or monetary payment, which will help reinforce your words.

Planning the Next Meeting

At the end of the meeting, it's a good idea to talk briefly about plans for the next meeting and ask if anyone wants you to cover anything else. By planning ahead, you can make your next meeting more productive.

Through planning, you'll have a better idea of what's important to cover, plus you'll involve your people in the process, which not only provides good ideas but motivation and commitment.

Also, if you are working with part-timers, whose schedules change frequently, check to see that most of the group plans to attend the next meeting. If not, depending on circumstances, it may be better to reschedule that particular meeting, or perhaps find another mutually convenient time for regular meetings.

If you are planning dates, a hand vote might be sufficient if most people agree. Otherwise, send around a sign-up list indicating different meeting days and times so people can express their preferences. At a break during the meeting, or while people are socializing afterward, you can review the suggestions and announce the most preferred day and time before people leave. Alternatively, you can call everyone later. And if necessary, you can schedule two meetings, which is better than not meeting at all with the people who can't make the original date.

PREPARING AN AGENDA

In order to have an effective meeting, regardless of your purposes, you need an agenda. That means you should work out in advance exactly what you want to cover and in what sequence. Also, it is important to write it down so you have a clear outline of everything you plan to cover.

With a small group, a written agenda for your own use is fine. Though, as your group gets larger, consider making copies of your agenda for everyone. This lets everyone know what you are going to cover, so they can let you know their suggestions for additions before the meeting.

I've included some examples of some of my own agendas to give you an idea of how I organized them. Below are highlights of my agenda activities:

Started out with a general update and passed out new materials. As part of this update, I included new flyers and masters, press releases and copies of ads or articles which appeared, new lead lists, copies of sample letters, scripts, price comparisons, and suggested marketing approaches.

Asked for feedback from people at some point in the meeting. In particular, I was interested in finding out what was working and what problems, if any, people were having. Then, we worked on resolving the problems collectively.

Asked people to tell me what they needed from me in terms of handouts, promotional materials, lead lists, marketing approaches, and so on.

Went over sales strategies. This discussion included going over a suggested telephone script for initial calls, discussing where people should go to find leads in their own community, ways to approach different types of people in different settings (in shops, churches, local civic and service clubs, bookstores, restaurants, friends, associates, neighbors).

Reviewed some of our joint experiences to consider what we could learn from them, such as comments and reactions on a trade show attended by six people in the group.

Coordinated day-to-day operations of the office by going over such things as using folders and files, recording messages in the telephone book, and reviewing record-keeping on various forms. I also passed around a sign-up form for people who wanted to use the office or meeting room.

Worked out plans for the group's participation in an upcoming trade show and scheduled individual participation in the company booth.

Demonstrated new products by showing clips from new videotapes. Those who wanted to view the films returned later.

Concluded the formal meeting with a discussion of the upcoming meeting and rechecked whether the time was good for everyone.

Put on sales training tapes for those who wanted to stay for this part of the meeting. Then, held a general discussion about how we could apply these principles to selling our particular program.

Organizing the Agenda

You need the structure of the agenda, so you can get where you're going. Otherwise, it's easy to get disorganized and ramble, and find a directed, productive sales meeting turning into a social chat or gossip session. But be flexible. In the course of the meeting, you may want to shift topics around, as a result of conversation and issues that come up.

Don't cover every possible topic in every meeting. Be aware of what you can do at a meeting, and use your agenda to organize the topics you want covered in the order in which you want to cover them.

How do you go about organizing an agenda? The night before a meeting, I go over what's new that I want to talk about, sales ideas I have had, problems I have noticed, and so forth. Essentially, I review the list of key functions mentioned at the beginning of this chapter and see if there is anything I have to say on these topics.

As I think of things I want to cover, I write them down in no particular order. It's really a form of the brainstorming, getting as many ideas as you can about a particular topic. Next, after I have all these ideas down, I rearrange them and decide which are the most important.

Typically, these are the topics I'll cover first. Then, I'll go on to less important matters. That way, if the discussion of important topics goes on longer than expected I can cut short the discussion of less important issues that come later, or perhaps drop them entirely.

Finally, I write my agenda in a more final form for presentation the next day. The agenda helps me organize by indicating materials I will need, such as brochures, flyers, or video-tapes. I get everything I need together so it's all ready the next day when I begin the meeting.

Sample Agenda, First Day

1. Update on past week
   Press releases
   Advertising for new people
   Organizational plans
   Leads from Marge
2. Sales strategies
3. Incentive/premium script
4. Finding leads yourself in your area
   Shops
   Churches
   Bookstores
   Camera shops
   Travel/luggage shops
   Ethnic shops with handicrafts of area
   Local Rotary, Lions, and other civic and service clubs
   Local high school/elementary school teachers
   Meetings, events to go to (bring flyers)

Restaurants and coffee houses (especially ethnic)

People you know who have been on trips

Friends, associates, neighbors who like your product or service, maybe invite them to a presentation at your house, show videos, or invite them here

Friends who work in large companies which may have incentive, premium programs

5. Feedback on what people are doing

What works

Any problems

What's needed from me

Future plans, meetings

Sample Agenda, Second Day

1. New handouts

Sample price comparisons

Approaching environmental groups

2. Comments, reactions on video

3. New files

Travel folders

For travel associations/for contacts

Telephone book for messages/message file

Group contacts form

4. New sources for leads

Better Business Bureau Book

Singles directory, new one in March

5. Additional places to suggest

Laundromat bulletin boards

Supermarket bulletin boards

Bookstores/magazine shops

Hotels

6. Reports by group members

Ellen on office/leads follow-up

Tom on environmental groups

Other?

7. New Films

On China, time to see them?

On Kenya, *Feathered Swarm; Rhino on the Run*

8. Use of office/meeting room?

9. Needs from me
   Flyers?
   China article?
   Press materials?
   Follow-up?
10. Recent press listings/ads
    Livermore Herald
    Gentry Magazine
11. Other
    Status of Tuesday meeting for next week
12. Sales training tapes by nationally known speakers

CONDUCTING THE MEETING

Let your sales people know that the beginning of the meeting is designed for them to chat and have coffee. But make the starting time clear, and start on time or at least no more than 5 to 10 minutes late if people are straggling in.

When you're ready, announce that the meeting is starting. Speak firmly and clearly and wait until you have everyone's attention before beginning. With a group of four or five people, you can be informal, leading it much like you would an ordinary conversation. As your group grows larger, I suggest a more formal style. For example, announce each item as you come to it, rather than casually moving from topic to topic.

If everyone knows each other, you can go right to the first item on your agenda. If some people are new or haven't seen each other before, take a few minutes for introductions, much like you would at an orientation, though briefer.

Getting Feedback

As you cover each item on your agenda, encourage comments from others, as appropriate, in addition to anything you have to say. The idea is to get others involved and participating, not just to give a one-sided report on the state of your company and its marketing plans.

To make people feel committed and creative, you have to help draw them out. Yet, at the same time, you still need to maintain control, bringing people back if they get off the track. Thank them for their comments and move on.

Participation. Another key to a good meeting is to encourage active involvement. Invite people to come up with ideas or solve problems for others. Be open and receptive. The essence of brainstorming is to invite ideas without initially criticizing them, which would slow the flow; it may even discourage them entirely. Then, after the idea creation process is over, you can winnow out those ideas that are really good.

Also, try to even out the conversation as people participate. If certain people talk a lot and dominate everyone else, find a diplomatic way to quiet them down, such as saying, "Well, that's a good idea. Now let's see what Donna or Archie has to say about that." Then, invite contributions from Donna and Archie or someone who hasn't said very much.

Timing. Be aware, too, of timing. Don't spend too much time on one topic and let the meeting run too long. Often people will have other commitments and not want to spend too much time at meetings. They make their money when they are out selling. Keep the meeting flowing and the discussion compact. If people bog down on one point, mention this and urge them to go on.

Plan the meeting to last a certain length of time, give or take a few minutes, and organize your agenda and the time you give each topic accordingly. Then, when people leave, they will feel a sense of satisfaction at having been at a tight, well-organized, productive meeting.

Controlling. The first rule for feedback is to make sure that it is positive. People should know this. It's fine to raise problems with a view to having the group as a whole solve them. But general criticism should be off limits. If people have general gripes, they should take them up privately with you and the others who might be involved, possibly in a special meeting. But none of this should come up in a general meeting.

Why? Because griping can cast a negative tone on the meeting as a whole and kill people's enthusiasm and motivation. Remember the key to successful selling is staying positive.

Finally, try to bring a feedback session to a close so people feel that issues have been resolved or that you are going to take into consideration the various points of view expressed when you make your decision later.

For example, if there seems to be a general consensus, tie things together by pointing this out. Or if there isn't, indicate that you plan to review all of the comments and decide something soon. This makes people feel their ideas are going to lead to action, and that the meeting has been useful and productive.

Brainstorming Sales Approaches

Regular sales meetings can be used very effectively to come up with new sales ideas by brainstorming. The process is divided into two stages. In the first, you come up with as many ideas as you can, without trying to evaluate or critique them. In the second, you go through the ideas and decide which you want to eliminate and which are viable. Then, depending on circumstances, you can make up a list of all the viable options and each person can choose what to do. Or you can discuss the pros and cons of the viable options as a group and make group decisions about what approaches to use.

Generating ideas. To get people to come up with ideas, first explain the process you will be using. Let people know you want them to throw out as many ideas as possible in the first stage without being critical. Point out that you will be evaluating these ideas in the second stage and determining which ones should be turned into a blueprint for action.

After explaining this, ask a question about the topic you want to find out about. For example, you might ask something like, "What types of groups should we approach?" or "How many ways can we let people know about our product?"

Then, encourage people to describe their ideas very quickly, so they don't have a chance to judge them. Whatever they think of, they should say. As each idea is presented, write it down or have someone else do it. Again, don't make any judgments as to what's good or not at this stage, just write everything down.

Evaluating the ideas. Next, review the list of ideas. One way to do this in a group is to read off each item and have people raise their hands if they think it's a good, useful idea. Then, if you see that all or most people agree, give it a double star. If about half or a substantial number agree, give it a check. If there's only one person or just a few who support it, indicate this with a question mark. And finally, if no one seems to like it, cross it off.

Now, you can take this priority list and as a group discuss the sales ideas you would most like to work with. Or if people are going to be working independently, simply type up the list with these suggestions. People can select on their own what they would like to do most.

An Example of Marketing Ideas

You can see how this process works from the following list of marketing ideas. It's a list of ideas compiled in a meeting where one person wanted to push a certain trip to environmental and nature groups. The person was relatively new in sales and wondered how to approach such groups.

I asked the group as a whole. What could he do? Then, after some brainstorming, I wrote up a list of the most promising ideas and made it available to everyone in the sales group. After all, other members of the group might want to contact environmental and nature groups.

Focus on wildlife in Kenya.

Use special programs and presentations with films.

Marketing approaches: distribute flyers through nature-oriented stores, schools and organizations; involve managers or leaders and members; gain their sponsorship; perhaps arrange a video-program/slide show to be held there.

Some examples of stores: mountaineering stores, camping, ski, and sports stores, camera stores, travel/luggage stores, safari clothing stores (Banana Republic).

Restaurants with a community/student atmosphere, for example, vegetarian restaurants, or restaurants near a campus.

Teachers in elementary schools, high schools, or colleges.

Theaters playing nature-oriented films.

Environmental organizations.

Special nature-oriented events, such as Wildlife Rehabilitation Conference.

Make arrangements with leaders in advance about fund-raising possibilities.

Go yourself and put out flyers or hand out to members.

Attempt to be included as a speaker or have video tapes included.

Ask to be an exhibitor and try to trade for free space with commissions or trip credit.

Stand outside as people leave or enter and give them flyers.

Churches/religious groups with nature-oriented groups.

Some nature groups to include: Sierra Club, Friends of the Earth, Outdoor Adventuring .

Museums/collections emphasizing nature, e.g., Academy of Sciences, Oakland Museum, San Francisco Zoo, Safari schools in Los Gatos

Wearing buttons, such as "Ask me about an African Safari" or "Want to Go Wild? Ask me."

Wearing T-shirt, "African Safari Adventures."

Maybe involve well-known local naturalists, environmentalists.

Maybe they'd like to be a leader, or their names would be enough of a draw to plan a free trip for them as part of a much larger group.

Creating Action Plans

Sales meetings are good for working out specific action plans for the group and getting people to make a commitment to them.

The action plan process works well in conjunction with brainstorming sales approaches. Essentially it involves taking a general approach such as, "Let's do cold calling downtown," and then working out the specific activities required to achieve the goal. It's like breaking down any procedure into the specific steps necessary to achieve a goal.

Example: a cold-calling plan. Say you've decided cold calling would be a good idea. What you would do, on your own or with the group as a whole, is decide what steps you need to take when, where, and who's going to take them. Thus, you would need to decide things like:

What part of the downtown should be used?
What streets or buildings should be included?
When shall we do this? What day and time?
What should we say?
What kind of presentation should we make?
What should we bring to make the presentation more effective?
Who will coordinate where we meet afterward?

Action planning process. When you're doing action planning in a group, simply develop a list of the questions you want answered in making your plan and then throw these out for discussion.

Encourage people to express their ideas, but stay in control of the discussion. After you get the flavor of what the group is thinking, seek to achieve a consensus, bring the issue to a vote, or announce what seems to be the best decision yourself, based on listening to what others say.

The idea is to consider possibilities, but then when one seems to be the strongest, quickly narrow down the possibilities so you can resolve each question with a decisive conclusion about how to act. Then, when you have answers to your questions, each one representing a part of your plan, you have a comprehensive plan of action.

Getting commitments. Besides planning action, you can use these meetings to get a commitment to action. One way, after creating an action plan, is to get each person involved to agree to a certain role, such as, "I'll reproduce the flyers so we can hand them out downtown."

Or, if people are acting independently, perhaps get a commitment to a specific goal for the week and to the specific plans they have made to make that goal happen. For instance, you might ask a person to make a commitment to make ten calls a day and spend two hours making presentations.

When you ask for such commitments it is very effective to get people to make the agreement out loud in front of the group. This way, everyone hears and there is a feeling of commitment to carry through on what is promised. Otherwise, if one person doesn't do this, he or she will lose face in front of the group.

Such a commitment isn't foolproof, because people can always appear the following week with an excuse. But with everyone else listening, they are less likely to do this or to make a commitment they can't fulfill.

Another way to get commitments is to use a sheet of paper with a statement of agreement or a certificate, in which the person pledges to do a certain thing. In this case, you should stress that the people are making the commitment to themselves; so if they don't keep it, then, they are only harming themselves. Once people understand the nature of this self-commitment, you can hand out the statement of agreement or certificate and ask them to sign it.

In the group situation, you can have several people each make a personal commitment and sign their own agreements at the same time. In this case, everyone's doing just what the individual person did, but again, the group-made commitment could be much firmer than the one made alone, simply because of the power of the group.

Setting up Incentives

The sales meeting can be an excellent format for recognizing what people have done and for developing incentives to do even more. (The use of awards is discussed in more detail in a later chapter.) Use the regular meeting to recognize ongoing achievements on a continuing basis. Also, note if there are areas where people are slacking off and create new incentives to get people to do more.

For example, when people give their weekly reports on activities you might give out small awards or gifts from time to time to recognize those who have achieved or surpassed certain goals. Say the previous week someone set a goal of making ten calls a day, resulting in five presentations a week and one big sale. The sale is certainly a reward. But perhaps, under certain circumstances, such as this being the person's first big sale, it might be a good idea to add to the reward. People will feel even more motivated to do more.

Another possibility is to use the sales meeting to find out what people expect to accomplish and when. You can develop this information into an incentive plan. For example, when people talk about their goals, use this to set up markers of achievement; then when people reach them later, you'll have a special award for them already planned.

On the other hand, if people aren't doing as well as expected, and you feel they can do better, announce that you have a new reward for anybody who achieves a certain goal. For instance, if people aren't putting enough emphasis into selling a certain product which normally sells well, sweeten the pie by offering a larger commission for a certain period; or provide an extra bonus for anyone who moves a minimum volume by a certain time.

Incorporating Sales Training Into the Meeting

Sales meetings are good for general sales training. However, I suggest making such training optional when you're working with part-time sales people. You'll find that some people, especially those new to sales, will be extremely interested in a good training program; in fact, it may be a factor in their decision to work with you.

On the other hand, some people, generally those with more experience, will feel they have heard it all; they'd rather spend their time in the field selling.

And then, there are those people who do have a great deal of experience but feel they can always learn more from additional training, since everyone has a slightly different approach.

Since people differ in how they feel about training, I suggest letting them know that you're willing to train and encourage them to participate. But then leave it up to them. To make participation easy but optional, you might hold general training sessions of about one half to one hour before or after the regular meeting.

13
Setting up a Training Program

A training program, held separately or in conjunction with regular sales meetings, can help your sales people perform more effectively. Most new sales people need training, and in part may be attracted to work with you because you offer it. Experienced sales people also can benefit from a good refresher course.

While conducting these sessions, you may acquire new ideas yourself, which you can incorporate into your overall sales strategy. In addition, a training program can be a source of inspiration and motivation, as your people get together on a regular basis to work on ways to sell better.

There are three key methods of training that you can use individually or in combination, depending on the needs of your group. First, you can use written materials, including books, articles, checklists, cassette tapes and video tapes, to provide instruction on sales techniques or product information.

Second, you can use role playing, setting up situations sales people may encounter, so they can practice good approaches and responses. Finally, you can act as a role model yourself, accompanying sales people into the field to show them how to sell, and observing them so you can offer feedback.

INDIVIDUAL VERSUS GROUP TRAINING

When you are first getting started and have only a handful of people working with you, individual training probably makes the most sense. On an as-needed basis, you can meet with sales people individually for role playing or accompany them on sales calls.

But once you have three or four people, it makes sense to shift to group training. For one thing, you'll find yourself stretched in too many directions if you try to train everyone individually. Second, at this stage you'll find that the peer group effect takes over, and your sales people will be motivated to improve their sales skills because others are doing it.

If you find that some people need extra attention, you can always set up separate meetings or go out on sales calls with them. Likewise, if some people aren't able to attend a meeting, you can always fill them in later or let them go through the sales-training materials on their own.

SETTING UP THE PROGRAM

Training programs that are flexible in format and content work best. Making a training program optional also works well, for several reasons. It's important to regard sales training separately from required sales meetings. Sales meetings are designed to pass out product information, coordinate what everyone is doing, and keep the group together.

If you do combine the sales meeting and training, you probably will want to keep the training session on the short side (for example, I found a half hour worked well). If training is separate, an hour to an hour and a half is probably fine.

Being Flexible

Sales training is designed to help individuals improve their abilities. People should therefore decide for themselves if they need improvement. Good sales people usually appreciate the importance of continued training.

Consider how you can apply training instruction to the products or services your sales people will be selling in the field. For example, if you're using generic sales training materials, include a discussion of how these can be adapted to the particular situations your people encounter.

Or use training sessions as a time to discuss sales methods that have worked well for you, encouraging others to share their ideas.

Another approach to involve your sales people more actively in the training process is to have them take turns leading training sessions. They can lead the discussion after a tape or video, or perhaps report on materials they have read, discussing how others can use these techniques.

Getting Feedback

From time to time, to see if you are on the right track, you should ask for feedback on your training. You may want to use a questionnaire to ask:

What sales techniques would they like to learn? What sales approaches are they having trouble with? Do they need help in locating leads?

Take the comments you receive to heart, and make any changes you think would improve the training offered in your group. You'll see the results down the road in the form of better trained sales people and better sales.

Also ask what kind of training approach people prefer. Do they like meeting in a group? Would they like to work more closely with you? How much time would they like to devote to training?

The key to setting up a good training program is being aware of what your people need and adapting it in format, content, and schedule.

USING WRITTEN MATERIALS, TAPES, AND VIDEOS

In your training sessions you can use materials you develop yourself, based on your own experiences in selling. Or you can draw on a wealth of books, articles, tapes, and videos developed by professional sales trainers who hold workshops and seminars all over the country.

The kind of materials you use depends on how experienced your people are. For instance, if you have a number of new people, it might be good to start with a step-by-step program.

Naturally, they will be selling while the program is being taught. But a training program will help them improve and can be used as a framework for discussing difficulties that come up in the field.

Video and Audio Tapes

Listening to a tape or watching a video in a group is ideal because it permits group discussion. However, to keep people attentive, limit any tape or video to no more than 15 to 30 minutes.

It's also a good idea for you to listen to such materials first, noting the main points to be discussed afterward. This discussion is important, because it helps underline the key things to learn from the tape. Also, it gives you and your sales people a chance to discuss how to apply the techniques in the field.

Printed Training Materials

If you use books or articles, a good approach is to arrange for everyone to read a chapter or a few articles in advance of the meeting.

Then, at the meeting you can go over the main points, based on what people have read. As in discussing tapes or videos, focus on how people can apply these techniques themselves.

Customized Training Materials

You can, of course, create your own sales-training materials. You might write up your ideas on a handout, which you can copy and distribute at the meeting. This is especially appropriate if you take techniques which you think are valuable and give examples of ways to apply them in the field.

For instance, if your sales people are going to follow up on ads or participate in a trade show, you might put together a list of good telephoning techniques to use in following up on leads.

ROLE PLAYING

Role playing, in which you set up a simulated situation and have participants act it out, is an excellent way to try out new techniques and practice old ones.

Begin by explaining what you are going to do and how role playing works. Note that participation is optional, so people don't feel they are suddenly on the spot to perform. Stress that the technique is valuable and that they are encouraged to participate. Most will.

Once people are prepared to try the technique, find out what sales areas your people feel they need help with, or use the technique to demonstrate how to do something new. For example, if people are having trouble making a cold call or making a close, set up some sample situations for role playing.

Setting the Stage

Once you have decided on the topics, select one and describe the situation. Probably it will just involve two participants, the sales person and the customer, though it can be more complex. When you set the stage, keep the description brief, so that participants can be spontaneous in playing out their roles as they see fit.

Start by reviewing the situation: for example, the sales person is calling a business executive to sell a new computer management service, and has just been put through by the secretary.

Showing How It's Done

If your sales people haven't played roles before, demonstrate how the process works by playing the sales person yourself and choosing another person to be the customer.

You can also demonstrate effective telephone selling by playing the role of the sales person yourself. Simulate how you would go about making the call, telling the other person to respond appropriately. Show how you open, what you do to keep interest, how you answer objections, and how you close in seeking to set up a meeting.

HavingThem Do It

After the demonstration, describe briefly what you did, highlighting the techniques you want your sales people to learn. Then, ask for volunteers to try out the exercise. A good technique is to ask participants to play out the situation once, switch roles, and do it again.

Ask the sales person to start the call, mentioning that the purpose is to set up a personal meeting with the executive to demonstrate the system. Encourage participants to improvise.

Evaluating the Results

An important part of role playing in training is getting reactions from the role players and observers, including yourself. In this way you learn how comfortable the "sales person" felt using certain sales techniques, how the "customer" reacted, and how observers felt about the "sales person's" approach and effectiveness.

After the role playing is over, typically with a sale, ask the "sales person" and the "executive" to talk about the experience. How did the "sales person" feel about the call? What was the goal? Was the exchange comfortable? What was uncomfortable, if anything? What worked? What didn't?

Then ask the "customer" for comments and reactions. What was good or not good about the approach? How did the sales person handle objections? Did the "executive" feel like setting up an appointment? Why or why not?

If the participants switched positions, ask them about both roles. Also, ask those who watched what they thought and felt. Finally, give your own reactions.

You might also talk about how the sales person might make it better; Perhaps the same people can play the situation again, using the ideas from the discussion to improve. Replays can be followed up with further discussion.

Replaying the Roles

If you feel it's appropriate, ask the same participants to do the simulation again, incorporating what they have learned from the discussion. Afterward, briefly discuss what they did.

Presumably, the scenario will be much more on target, so there will be less to discuss. Mostly, this is just a time to affirm that the sales person is making a better presentation and the customer is more responsive as a result.

Next, ask for more volunteers to play out the same scene. If you prefer, suggest modification: "Okay, the same situation as before, but this time, the customer is an extremely busy person," or "Okay, the same situation as before, but this time, the customer wants to get all the answers on the phone instead of meeting with you in person."

Try out a few more situations in a similar fashion. At the end, ask people to discuss what they learned from the role-playing session, and summarize the main points. Finish by asking if anyone has suggestions for situations to role play next time.

When to Stop

How much time should be spent on role playing? It depends on your situation and the response of people in your group. Some sales people will feel comfortable with the technique and may have used it before; they like the chance to try out new approaches and get feedback.

Other sales people may resist it, either because they feel uncomfortable about being on stage in front of their peers, or they feel they already know how to sell. Many will simply go along with whatever you decide to do. Taking a reading of your group's interest will help you decide how much time to spend.

Assuming the people in your group are responsive, about 15 to 30 minutes is usually a good length of time for role playing as part of a regular training session. It permits time for both acting out scenes and for some discussion. If you set up a special role-playing workshop, one to two hours is a good length of time.

ACTING AS A ROLE MODEL IN THE FIELD

A third training method is acting as a role model yourself by accompanying sales people in the field. Alternatively, you can use other experienced sales people to accompany those being trained.

The strength of this approach comes from the hands-on experience. Some experienced sales people may not need this, but it's ideal for new people and for those who haven't sold your kind of product or service before. It is also helpful if you have developed special approaches for selling.

Commonly, the role-model technique involves three stages: the new person as observer only, joint participation, and the new person making the presentation with support.

The New Person as Observer Only

In this stage, you or another experienced sales person takes the newcomer out in the field as an observer. The newcomer is introduced as your assistant.

The number of presentations newcomers should observe before starting to sell depends on their previous experience and on your product or service. If your product or service is fairly complex, say a computer system, you may want the person to observe in the field several times before sharing in the presentation or doing it alone. With a simple program, a one-time observation may be sufficient. Experienced people will need less of an introduction; a novice in sales will need much more.

Warning the prospect. If you are demonstrating cold-calling techniques, obviously no special advance introduction to customers is necessary. Simply bring the newcomer along as your assistant. If you are making a presentation by appointment, let the prospective customer know in advance that you are bringing your assistant with you.

It is a matter of courtesy to let prospects know what to expect, so they can be prepared and perhaps have an extra chair in the office. An advance warning is not absolutely necessary, but it shows respect for the prospect, and may create a more receptive atmosphere.

Procedure. If you're working with telephone techniques, let the new person listen in on the call. Before any type of sales call it helps to give the new person an idea of what to expect. This will help emphasize the specific techniques you use.

At a presentation, a newcomer should only observe. It's all right to ask for minor assistance such as putting up charts or getting out presentation material. Newcomers should not ask any questions or offer any information. Be clear about that, because you don't want interference with your presentation, possibly derailing the sale.

After each presentation or after the last presentation, hold a short discussion or debriefing session. Discuss what you did. Explain why you used certain techniques. Encourage newcomers to ask questions and and give reactions.

Some sales leaders debrief in the car while driving to and from appointments or returning to the office. But it's preferable if you can set a special time to focus on this discussion, perhaps over coffee at the end of the day.

Joint Participation

In this stage, the newcomer gradually assumes more and more responsibility for the sales call. Discuss the presentation beforehand to find out what the newcomer feels most comfortable doing.

Reserve for yourself the more critical parts of the presentation, for example, the opening and the close. Plan who is going to do what and stick to this in the presentation, which will flow more smoothly if you both are certain of what to do.

You might start off by having the newcomer provide limited support activities, such as demonstrating your product or service after you make a brief introduction. Also, if you are using a presentation folder, flip charts, overheads, or other similar materials, you might have the newcomer manipulate them while you explain.

Once the new sales person feels comfortable with limited support activities, you can begin turning over more of the presentation. Through this process you can shift more and more of the presentation until the newcomer feels comfortable handling the whole thing. Your confidence in that person will rise at the same time.

After the presentation, allow time for discussion and feedback. In particular, point out what was good and what could be improved. If the person makes mistakes, be supportive. Point them out in a constructive way to show how to improve next time.

Ask how the new person feels about what happened, both likes and dislikes. Also, ask what changes the person would like to make in the future. The point of the discussion is to help new people get better and be prepared to take on more responsibility the next time.

One or two joint participation presentations may be enough for some newcomers; others may need more. Again, it depends on the product or service and the background of the new people. Use feedback and your own judgment to help you decide.

Giving a Presentation with Support

This stage provides an opportunity to refine the presentation and to make it even better. You, or an experienced sales person, are the observer. The newcomer does the whole thing. You might assist a little, such as demonstrating the product or service or turning the flip chart, but otherwise it's the new person's show. You are introduced as the assistant.

Use this opportunity to observe closely. Notice how the new person does the opening, maintains interest, creates rapport with the customer, deals with objections, and handles the close. After the presentation, offer your reactions on strengths and areas for improvement, and ask how things went.

If you both feel the presentation went well, the new person may be ready to go out alone. Or perhaps you might both do one more presentation with support, just to be sure.

Play it by ear in deciding when new people are ready. Your goal should be to get them off on their own as quickly as possible.

Commissions

On any sales that result from an experienced sales person's usual presentation in showing a newcomer what to do, the experienced person should get full credit.

Once the new sales person starts setting up appointments and making presentations, with the experienced person helping, it seems fair to split the commission 50/50.

Or an override system can be used, in which the person is assigned to the supervision of an experienced sales person, who gets an override on all of the new person's sales.

14
Coordinating Sales Activities

When you first organize a sales group, many aspects can be left loose and informal. You still aren't sure how your few new people are going to work out. At the same time, you should have the basics of organization in mind, so you can gradually introduce them to your group as the circumstances seem right.

In this chapter, I describe a number of organizational procedures. Choose those that feel comfortable for your style and the stage of your organization's development. You may want to mention in advance some of the procedures you plan to use later, so people will be ready to accept them when they are introduced.

AVOID OVERLAPPING CONTACTS

A primary concern in any sales group is the problem of coordinating contacts. Your sales people will probably welcome any coordinating you do, since duplicate contacts become a major problem as a sales force grows.

As a practical matter, when there are several sales people in a local area, it is important to set up guidelines, if not territories or categories. At the least, you should establish some general policies about how to handle joint contact situations, so people know who gets the commission for a sale and feel it's fair.

For example, if one person makes the contact and the other closes the sale independently, you might split the commission, so long as the closing occurs reasonably soon after the original contact.

Let the Sales People Decide

One good approach to setting up territories or categories when you are first getting started is to let the decision come from the new people you hire. You might begin with a general idea of how you want to organize a sales force within an area (downtown, certain neighborhoods, outlying areas), or by category (business and professional groups, singles and social groups, nature and environmental groups, factories, Spanish-American community). Then get a sense of what your people want to do themselves and modify your plan accordingly.

One way to find out what new people want is to ask when you interview them. In fact, your hiring decision may be partly based on having a mix of people working in different geographic or interest areas. Another way is to ask your people to fill out a questionnaire every six months or so, to see if their interests have changed.

Ask such questions as, "What neighborhoods in the city would you like to work in?" "What types of groups do you currently belong to?" "What types of groups or companies would you prefer to contact?" As you review their answers, you can decide how tò assign people to previously or newly created categories.

Be Flexible

It's good to leave arrangements fairly flexible at first. Perhaps let people know how you have recorded their primary areas of sales effort, and let everyone know who is working in which area. As it becomes clearer who is doing what, you can gradually create firmer boundaries between areas (that is, dividing up the city by specific streets, or specifying that one person will be handling all the churches in a city). Certainly allow for exceptions (for instance, one person has close friends in someone else's area), and invite feedback at sales meetings.

As long as you take the interests of your people into consideration in setting up the system, you will find that they like the idea of having some structure. Otherwise they may waste time contacting someone who was already contacted by another sales person. Or they will get into disputes about who gets the commission, which can easily create hard feelings.

Keep a Record

Another approach to avoid overlap is to have sales people fill out a contact form listing each company or organization they are actively working with in a specific category or area. An example of a contact form is shown on the next page.

Create a Filing System

To file these contact forms so others can refer to them, set up a filing system according to sales person and by the categories or areas of contact. You can use ordinary manila folders or hanging files with labels for this purpose.

Group Contact Form

Please fill out this form for each business or group you are actively in contact with, so you can be appropriately credited, should someone from this organization contact the office directly. This form can be used to avoid or resolve any problems that may arise from multiple contacts of the same group. It can also be used for general follow-up by the office.

Your name
Name of group leader/contact
Name of individual, group or company
Type of group & special interests
Address
City, State, Zip
Phone
(home, office, when best to call)
Date of first contact
Outcome
Products/services interested in

Additional follow-up on back of form (date, outcome, topics discussed, special interest, etc.)

File the master under the person's name, and file a copy alphabetically by either category, geographical area, or both. Other people in your group can then refer to these files to see who not to contact.

When your group is small, you can simply share this information at a meeting. But as the group grows, you will need to keep a list of the names, addresses, and phone numbers of everyone in your group, where they are working, and their areas of special interest.

If you are considering such a system, check with your people first to see that this is acceptable. It does require a certain amount of paperwork and filing. Some people may not like to do this or may be lackadaisical about keeping these forms up to date. You need the support of your people to make the system work.

SET UP A MESSAGE SYSTEM

Telephone message and mail coordination is another service you can provide to your sales people. Some of them may prefer to work independently and use their own phones and mailing addresses. Others will want to use your office as a base.

If you have a receptionist or answering service, taking calls and messages is easy. If you're just starting, you may need to use an answering machine instead. In that case, it's worth investing in another phone to be used solely for taking business calls.

When you prepare your message, I suggest including these elements to sell your program and make messages clearer:

Name of your company.
Brief description of the products or services you offer.
Brief mention of available presentations or sales demonstrations.
Request to leave a name, phone number, reason for call, and best time to return it.
Request that callers specify the particular person they are trying to reach.
Statement that someone will return the call as soon as possible.
Reminder to be sure to name the particular person being called.

Following is an example of a message we used very effectively with our travel sales group. Callers usually left a message and often specified who it was for.

Sample Telephone Message

"Hello. You have reached Creative Travel. We are currently offering trips to Kenya, China, Egypt, Greece, and Morocco. We will be adding trips to Australia, New Zealand, Fiji, Tahiti, and Tibet this spring. We are also putting on regular travel nights around the Bay Area, and if you would like us to put on a presentation for your group or organization, please let us know. We offer group and individual trips.

"At the beep, please leave your name, what you're calling about, and which Travel Associate you want to reach. Please tell us the best time to get back to you. If you want us to send you information, please leave your address and the destinations you are interested in. Someone will be in touch with you as soon as possible."

Distribute Leads Accurately

Identifying a sales person for each lead is important so you can give appropriate sales credit. That's the reason for stressing that callers should name the person they are calling. Since sales people get paid by a commission when a sales comes through, be very careful to record this information accurately. This is critical for good coordination and keeping your sales people satisfied that the message system is working well.

When callers don't specify who they want, return the call and try to find out. If they don't know where they heard of your product, probe to find out (business card at a mixer, poster on a wall, flyer at a meeting) and where or when this occurred. This will help you figure out who was responsible for the materials. If you can't determine the source, treat it as an unsolicited lead and distribute it to whoever is handling those companies or groups or is covering that particular geographic area.

Take the messages off the tape yourself on a regular basis. You're in the best position to do this since you are the coordinator. This also avoids a sales person being tempted by a call to take someone else's lead.

If a sales person isn't due to come into the office for awhile, you can call and pass on the message, or put it in that person's message file.

Setting Up a Separate Message File

A good approach for message taking is a message record book, sometimes called an "Executive Message Record." This permits messages to be taken in duplicate, using one page for the original message and an imprinted carbon and following page for the copy.

You can slip the original message into a message file, and still have a record of it. If the first message gets lost or the sales person doesn't act on it, you can always use the copy for follow up later.

As for the file itself, you can use manila folders with your sales people's names on them, filed alphabetically. Or use a hanging folder for each sales person with a series of separate manila folders in each one.

The important thing is to have some sort of organized message keeping system so that people efficiently get their messages, and you have a record of them in case some get lost or you need to follow up or reassign the message later.

The same system can be used for letters addressed to your sales people as well as messages from you.

DISTRIBUTING SALES MATERIALS

As you develop new sales materials, training aids, commission plans, and other information for your sales people, go over each item at a sales meeting to make sure everyone understands and feels comfortable with it. This is the time to listen to feedback and make any modifications necessary.

An efficient way to distribute sales materials at meetings is to pile them on a table at a central spot. Ask everyone to pick up a copy, saying that you will review everything at the meeting.

Besides this initial distribution, it's a good idea to have a file for such materials accessible to all of your people. The Crate-A-Files and collapsible hanging file systems mentioned earlier are ideal for this purpose. Create a folder for each item you distribute, label it, and place it in the file, with new materials in the front. Then, if someone misses material at a meeting, runs out, or needs a master to make copies, it is easily available.

The file can be organized into logical categories, using folders divided with tabs. Some typical categories might be ad copies, sample letters, masters for flyers, masters for stationery, articles, marketing policies and procedures, marketing ideas, order forms, newsletters.

Use a list of materials you have prepared and distributed to help your people know if they have everything. Update this every few weeks and keep a copy in the front of the file.

This kind of filing system is also useful when you bring on new people. It will help in gathering materials already passed out to others. Be sure to go over all of this information at the orientation for new sales people, as previously discussed.

USING A NEWSLETTER TO PASS ON INFORMATION

A newsletter for updates is an excellent tool, in addition to your regular sales meetings, for keeping a sales group informed. With only a handful of people, an update in memo form is fine.

As your group grows, a more formal newsletter with a special title looks more impressive. It can also be used to recruit new sales people, since it shows what you have been doing to support and guide your group.

Initially, you might do all the writing yourself. But as your group and newsletter grow, ask your sales people to contribute copy, such as, "Sales approaches that have worked for me."

Newsletter Topics

Some of the topics to cover in your newsletter updates include:

> Sales meeting dates, special topics to be covered.
> Dates of upcoming presentations, talks, and workshops of interest which you or others will give.
> Plans for new materials to be developed, and a request for suggestions on materials needed.
> New marketing and promotional materials available at the next meeting or in the sales materials file.
> Upcoming advertising.
> Highlights of a planned publicity approach.
> Arrangements for upcoming sales parties or special events.
> Availability of new brochures, flyers.
> Sales tips from recent meetings.
> List of new sales people or a welcome to newcomers.
> Guidelines for follow-up after a planned promotional event.
> Current commission arrangements.
> New products and services which are available.
> Reports of achievements of other sales people.
> Report on an awards or recognition program.

Newsletter Format and Frequency

Two to four pages is a good beginning length for your update or newsletter. You can create a nice looking letterhead or title using rub-on letters. By making master copies of your letterhead, you can type the newsletter on these sheets or paste up your copy directly on the master later. Use a short headline to introduce each topic so that key points will jump out at the reader.

Be sure to include a date, and also show that it is part of a continuing series by numbering each issue. Keep back copies to show new people to let them know what your company has been doing.

When you are first getting started, an issue every three or four weeks will suffice. As your group grows, add pages and bring it out more frequently, perhaps every two or three weeks.

GETTING FEEDBACK

It is important to get feedback from your group from time to time to help you coordinate their sales activities. Find out what people need so you can prepare the necessary materials or adapt your support activities.

One source of feedback, of course, is conversation with individuals, both day to day and during regular sales meetings. As part of every meeting, ask people what they need from you.

It can be helpful, particularly as your group grows, to develop materials to gather feedback, such as a feedback questionnaire or comment sheet. It provides a way for sales people to say what they want to. If they wish, their replies can be anonymous.

Questions to Ask

A comment sheet should ask these key questions:

What kind of additional materials do you need?

What kind of help would you like in sales training?

What types of obstacles or problems, if any, are you encountering in the field?

How can our sales meetings be more useful for you?

How do you like the newsletter/update? What else would you like to see included? What changes do you suggest? How often should it be published?

Do you need any help with leads? What other kinds of assistance would be helpful?

How do you feel about the way things are being coordinated? Do you have any suggestions for improvement?

You'll notice that these questions are designed to get feedback in a positive, constructive way. While some ask for comments about possible problem areas, they are designed to get suggestions for improvement.

When to Do It

One good way to get questionnaires filled out is to ask everyone to take ten minutes during a general meeting or bring them back at the next meeting. If you do this, be sure to stress the importance of bringing them back, because people commonly forget.

Using questionnaires may be good if people feel uncomfortable writing their comments during the sales meeting or in front of you. They may feel on the spot and prefer to turn in their responses anonymously. In this case, make up a file for them to put the sheets in.

However you distribute the comment sheets, it's important to emphasize the value of this feedback for the group as a whole, as well as for individuals. Point out that you will be using it to help members of the group, to prepare needed materials, and to make sales meetings better. Also, you want to know what changes are needed in the way you are coordinating things.

In short, your emphasis should be on using this material to improve things for everyone. Once sales people realize that this can help them, they will be more receptive.

Review the Replies

When you get the forms back, review them question by question to get a general sense of what people want. Note where a number of people mention the same wants or needs. For instance, you may be asked to develop certain materials, add other areas of sales training, or provide more leads.

If only one or two people make the same comment, it might be helpful to mention it at your next meeting, showing that you are aware of it. You can see if others express a similar need, and if so, respond accordingly. In any event, after you receive feedback you should report on the major comments and on how you plan to respond.

How often should you do this? That will depend on how things are going with your group. If things seem to be going smoothly, perhaps every four to six weeks is a good time to get organized feedback. Do it more often if you sense there are problems, or if you feel like you want to make changes.

15
Keeping Your Sales Group Motivated

Motivation is critical for effective selling. Sales people must be enthusiastic in taking the initiative to make contacts. And they need to maintain that enthusiasm to carry them through the sale.

Many prospects are going to say no, as many as 90 to 95% in some sales programs. In spite of this, sales people need to be able to put day-to-day obstacles aside and focus on their ultimate success in achieving their goals.

Some people are self-motivated, but many need assistance from their leaders or other sales people to stay on track. And those who are already motivated can use your assistance to do even better.

There are a number of things you can do to keep your sales people motivated, depending on the size of your sales group and their responsiveness to different approaches:

Use individual motivators on a regular basis.
Use meetings to motivate and inspire.
Offer awards and incentives to motivate performance.
Use special events to provide recognition.

INDIVIDUAL MOTIVATORS

This approach is ideal when a sales group is small, though you can continue to use it along with other methods as the group grows. The key is to show your personal interest, recognition, and approval on a one-on-one basis. Let people know you are really behind them and want to help.

Call Them Up

Make an occasional phone call to see how things are going. Do so in a positive way. Let people know you are not just checking up on sales.

Perhaps offer a suggestion for a new sales approach you have found effective. Or tell them about an upcoming talk, article on sales, or inspirational book they might find interesting.

Another possibility is to see if their sales approach or leads referral list is working well. If not, what can you do to improve the situation?

When you call your tone should be friendly and supportive. The call should be direct and to the point. The idea is not to chat, but to spark up people, get them excited and motivated to sell.

If there are any difficulties, this is the time to deal with them and try to improve the situation. If the problem is relatively simple, such as "What would be a good thing to say to get through the secretary?" you can probably handle it right then and there.

Meet to Discuss Problems

If it's something that needs talking over, such as "I'm having trouble locating and contacting non-profit groups. What do you suggest?" then set up an individual meeting to discuss it.

If you feel others have the same problem, bring it up at your next group meeting. Often such issues won't come up during a motivational call. But if they do, deal with them because they are a barrier to motivation.

Besides making calls, you can meet individually to show your support. This is also a good time to get general feedback on how people think things are going. Notice any criticism or complaints, and indicate that you would like to help improve the situation. Such meetings can be quite short, 10 to 30 minutes.

Typically, a meeting in your office or over coffee is fine. But if you want to say thanks for doing especially well, use the get together as a special occasion, perhaps treating the person to lunch or dinner.

MEETINGS TO MOTIVATE AND INSPIRE

Once a sales group is large enough for regular group meetings, motivational meetings become important. These can be held as special meetings or as part of your regular weekly sales meetings.

One type of meeting used by some sales leaders is the "sizzle session." These are small get-togethers, usually five to fifteen people and sometimes as many as twenty, which can include a mixture of inspiration, training, planning, brainstorming, and a little socializing.

The main purpose of these meetings is to create enthusiasm ("sizzle") and come up with plans and ideas. Participants should leave feeling charged up and ready to go.

Organizing Sizzle Sessions

You can organize sizzle sessions in various ways. One sales leader I know met with a few of his sales people in a restaurant, generally in midmorning or early afternoon. As people arrived they described something positive that happened with their sales efforts. Then, they shared ideas about how to create more sales.

Another possibility is to have a different person lead each meeting, rotating the responsibility. The leader's goal is to guide others in thinking up new sales strategies and solutions to problems.

However you run your meetings, the key to a good sizzle session is to keep everyone involved, thinking positively, and focusing on the topic at hand.

Avoid negative gossip. The emphasis should be on finding solutions, not on sharing problems. In this way everyone will feel a creative "sizzle" and be part of a warm, supportive, positive, dynamic group.

Using Motivational Speakers

Besides the "sizzle session," another kind of motivational meeting is one that features an inspirational and motivational speaker or discussion. Such meetings may be held occasionally or on a regular basis. At other times motivational sessions may be incorporated into regular meetings, perhaps for 15 to 30 minutes.

A good way to start off such a meeting is with a high-energy, positive activity. For example, I was once part of an organization where the leader, a real holy-roller type, began by asking people to introduce themselves with the statement: "I'm the Great So-and-So, and I'm (excited to be here ... going to sell $1,000 this week ... raring to go out and contact at least ten people today)."

The approach may sound corny but it worked. In fact, at some meetings, people outdid themselves in enthusiasm, because the leader offered a reward, usually a $20 or $50 bill, to the person who showed the highest energy. In one case, a man won by standing on his head as he told how motivated and enthusiastic he felt.

I don't necessarily recommend the "I am great" approach. But I think the idea of getting people's adrenaline going is a good one. It adds intensity to the motivation.

Motivating from Within

A more subdued way to achieve the same result might be to ask your own sales people to kick off a meeting by telling what they are really excited about doing right then or the next week.

Then, once everyone is in an enthusiastic and positive frame of mind, you can shift into the focus of the motivational meeting. Some good possible approaches for this include one or more of the following.

Show and tell. A good way to get everyone involved in motivating one another is to use a kind of motivational show and tell. For this, invite people to bring in anything they think is motivational: stories, poems, illustrations, photographs, ideas, and so on.

During the meeting, ask for volunteers to describe what they have brought in. For example, one person might volunteer to read a poem and share reactions; another might bring in a short book about being successful and read a few excerpts; another might describe a talk recently heard. Allow 10 to 20 minutes for this.

Report on a motivational book, article, or film. You can do this yourself, or have a volunteer do it. The person giving the report chooses a book, article, or film to review, and then reports on it at the meeting. However, this report should be more than a summary of what was read or seen.

The reviewer should personalize the report. What effect did it have? How could the message be applied so group members could become more successful in selling or in life generally? Plan on 5 to 10 minutes for each report.

Call on a speaker. Ask members to speak on a motivational subject for 10 to 20 minutes. Such topics can be related specifically to sales ("How I made my sales goals for the month" or "How to turn a no into yes.") Or the talk can deal with success themes generally, such as "Why being positive guarantees positive results."

Play a motivational tape or video. To hold attention, keep this to about 15 minutes for an audio tape or up to 20 to 30 minutes for a video. You can use either sales-related or general success-oriented topics, as noted above.

Discuss the message. You can lead this yourself or turn it over to a volunteer. The main purpose of this discussion is to get everyone in the group to react to the motivational message and think about how to apply it to themselves.

Each person in the group should be encouraged to say something. The leader might ask for volunteers or have everyone in the group say something in turn. Use the approach that feels most comfortable for your group. About 15 to 20 minutes is a good length for such a discussion.

Agenda for a Motivational Meeting

A representative motivational meeting about an hour long might go something like this:

> Opening kickoff: introductions, positive remarks (5 minutes)
> Motivational show and tell (10 minutes)
> Report on a motivational book (5 minutes)
> Motivational tape, video, or speaker (15 minutes)
> Discussion of the tape, video, or speaker (20 minutes)
> Final message of inspiration, song, cheering, etc. (5 minutes)

The possibilities for putting on creative, exciting motivational meetings are endless. The key is to keep everyone interested and involved by varying the pace, getting people to contribute, and making motivational ideas personal, so people see exactly how they can use these ideas themselves. Be sure to conclude motivational meetings on a positive, uplifting note, so people feel ready to take what they have learned and sell.

The Importance of Motivational Activities

Whether you use sizzle sessions, motivational meetings, or part of your regular meeting for motivational purposes, you should do something to keep your group as a whole motivated. Not only will your people find the content of the meeting helpful, but they will welcome your support. Furthermore they will stimulate each other to sell.

It may help to think of the benefits of the motivational meeting as a triangle with the sales person in the center. There are three sources of benefits: you, the meeting, and other sales people in the group.

MOTIVATING WITH AWARDS AND INCENTIVES

Other key motivators are awards and incentives. Most if not all sales organizations use them to recognize accomplishment and provide a goal for others. Such awards and incentives can become quite elaborate as companies get large, and the recognition ceremonies can be spectacular affairs.

Making a Big Splash

Mary Kay Cosmetics holds gala celebrations at exotic locations, where top performing beauty consultants are honored, and the highest achievers get the keys to a pink Cadillac. Other companies combine award ceremonies with elegant dances or parties. Some award cruises and vacations to their top sales people. In fact, there's a whole incentive travel industry that has emerged to wine, dine, and pamper successful sales people in luxurious vacation locations.

Still other companies have regular monthly award ceremonies, that combine recognition with tips to sales people. For example, in an award ceremony at a jewelry company, the master of ceremonies introduced the top performers of the month, and the crown of achievement was passed from the top sales person of the previous month to the new one. In addition, there were certificates and awards for those who had shown the greatest increase in sales, the most improvement, and the best attitude.

Some companies introduce special sales promotions, in which they offer extra commissions, gifts, premiums, and so forth for making certain sales goals during the period.

How to Start Small

If you are just getting started and only have a few sales people, you obviously can't go all out with pizzazz. But you should develop some kind of small program for awards or incentives and as your sales group grows, expand on it.

As you introduce different awards and incentives, notice which ones are most effective for your group and develop additional incentives of this type. For example, some people respond more to financial bonuses, others more to recognition in special events and ceremonies. Still others may be attracted by premiums, vacation packages, and trips.

Get a sense of how your group feels, and tailor your incentive program accordingly. Include questions about incentives on feedback questionnaires from time to time to get information about your group in this and other areas.

Stage One. Some possible incentives you can use in the earliest stages of developing your group include:

A financial bonus for making a certain sales goal by a certain time.
An increased commission rate for all sales made in a certain month.
A thank-you dinner or night on the town on the company.
A bonus gift for a certain sales volume in a given month.

You'll notice that this first level of incentives is essentially financial in nature or involves a bonus gift. That's because in the early stages, you don't have the group network established that makes recognition awards, ceremonies, and events so powerful.

Stage Two. As your group grows, you can start adding other types of incentives and rewards:

Award certificate (preferably framed).
Plaque or cup signifying a certain achievement level.
Listing of the award or achievement in your newsletter.
Biweekly or monthly awards program as part of your regular meeting.
Special party or meeting to honor top performers (perhaps every few months to start; eventually every month or two).
Specially made bonus gift, such as an engraved watch, leather bound book for photographs, personalized luggage.
Weekend trip to a nearby location associated with having fun, such as a trip to Las Vegas from San Francisco or to Atlantic City from Philadelphia.
Extra bonus and/or a big gift for having the highest sales volume or initiating the most new accounts.

Tailor the Reward

Be creative in deciding on appropriate awards. For example, relate an award to a sales person's particular interest. For example, if a person is a music buff, use tapes and records as the award.

Similarly, take into consideration the interests of your sales people in shaping an awards event. For instance, if you're selling jewelry, a glittery, elegant event might be appropriate. But if you're selling health items and your people tend to be more casual in style, maybe put on a picnic or an open air festival in a tent.

As your group grows, you might also consider getting a quantity of gift and premium items from an advertising specialty company. These companies are listed under "advertising specialties" in your local yellow pages. They feature all kinds of premiums and promotional items, including buttons, pens, key tags, glasses, mugs, certificates, T-shirts, trophies, executive gifts, and recognition awards. They will personalize these items with the name of your company or the name of the person getting the award.

For additional ideas about awards and incentives, ask people who are with other companies. Ask those in companies similar in size to your own or just a little bit larger for the most relevant information.

In sum, an awards and incentive program can help you to expand. It can stimulate your sales people to do that little bit more which can translate into increased commissions and recognition for them and increased sales and profits for you.

AWARD CEREMONIES AT REGULAR MEETINGS

When you first organize a sales group, you will be mainly concerned with giving recognition at regular meetings or at occasional evening ceremonies. Using a regular meeting to provide recognition is a good way to begin.

Save the awards until last, allowing a break between regular activities and the recognition/awards part. This way, whatever you do feels more special. You might also note on the agenda the time the regular meeting is to end and when the special award ceremony begins.

Make it Special

Play up the recognition, making that part of the meeting special, so the person getting the award feels in the limelight. Not only does this make people feel good, it helps motivate them. It can also motivate others in the group.

When it comes time to recognize achievement, create a little ritual. For instance, say a few words when you hand someone a certificate, premium, bonus check, gift, or whatever to show your appreciation. Point out what the person has done, and how. Perhaps ask the person to say a few words. Talking about the person's achievement is good, because this gives others guidelines for what they can do, as well as getting them to think about working harder to gain recognition, too.

If you are giving recognition to several people, save the person who is getting the highest recognition for last. That way you build up to the high point of the event. Finally, include time for conversation and refreshments. This is a good time for people to congratulate the person who has been recognized and ask about how it was done.

Create a Program Booklet

You can create a program booklet using your typewriter or word processor, which lists the people who are being recognized and their accomplishments. When you have only a few people, it may seem a little silly to do this. I have been at meetings where there was only a handful of people, so that it looked as though everyone were giving awards to everyone else. That doesn't matter. People still feel good about it, because they value the opinions of the others.

Serve Special Refreshments

Another way to liven up a small meeting is with special refreshments. For example, get a cake and embellish the icing with the name of the person being recognized. Perhaps put in candles for certain levels of sales volume attained, e.g., one candle for every $1,000. Maybe have champagne, and consider using buttons, streamers, or other party favors to create a celebration mood.

Another possibility is to invite people to bring their own dishes and turn the event into a potluck meal. Or maybe reserve a table in a nearby restaurant and move your celebration there.

Naturally, take into consideration the tastes and style of your own group. The point is to do something special so this isn't just a regular sales meeting. Instead, at least part of it has a flavor of ceremony and celebration, so the people being recognized feel honored and everyone can see you care about your group.

SPECIAL MEETINGS FOR AWARDS

If you're planning a separate event to provide recognition, the format can be similar. Just make the ceremony a little more elaborate and add a period of socializing or other highlights, such as speakers.

Different groups use different formats. Some start with dinner or a potluck meal. Others open with cocktails or have coffee and conversation. However you do it, plan on about a half hour for people to arrive and for socializing.

Then, if you have a program of any sort, have this before the awards. Save the recognition part of the program for last, so the occasion builds. Make the awards the real highlight. Build by giving out smaller awards first. Save the biggest one, such as "Sales Person of the Month" or "Sales Person of the Year," for last.

Jazz it Up

As you give out each award, describe the accomplishments, perhaps telling a little about the person ("You may be amazed at how much Sylvia can do when she really gets out there and decides to do it. Not only did she up her sales volume 50%, but she has a husband, two kids, a dog, and she is in a church singing group on the side.")

Then, prominently show the award you are giving out. If it's a certificate, hold it up and read it; if you or anyone has written a note of congratulations, read that too. Finally, if there are any symbols of recognition, give them out and let the recipients show them off.

For example, at his group's monthly awards program, a jewelry sales leader would take the crown of leadership from the previous month's winner and crown the new monthly sales winner. He would also put a red velvet cloak around her shoulders and the group photographer would take photos. These would go to the participants and to the newsletter.

Make a Record

You can arrange for someone in your group to take photographs of the occasion, and if you have a newsletter which uses photos, include them. Alternatively, include a report of the event and a listing of everyone who won awards.

You might even add to the occasion by having someone in your group provide musical accompaniment; perhaps have someone record it all on a video.

Following the program and ceremony, include time for socializing, or perhaps couple the event with a party or dance.

AWARDS ARE WORTHWHILE

You'll find that award events can be memorable and important to your sales people. Feeling genuinely recognized for their efforts, they are apt to try harder. At the same time, their recognition makes them role models for others in the group. Everyone usually leaves such events feeling good and more committed to the group.

Award and recognition ceremonies, organized occasionally, help keep everyone directed and motivated. They help everyone feel good about working together. In turn, this increases commitment, motivation, and good feeling, which translates into more sales.

16
Providing Extra Assistance and Support

In addition to providing training, coordination, and motivation, you can support your group with other forms of assistance to make it more effective. You can help with sales leads by developing sources yourself, coordinating their distribution, and helping people develop their own leads.

You can also develop sample telephone scripts, letters, and sales presentation guidelines to illustrate approaches you have found especially effective. You can offer tapes and videos or the opportunity to observe sales presentations. You can put on presentations or demonstrations to which your sales people can bring customers. You can create sales presentation books for your people or show them how to create their own. And you can get regular feedback from your people to find out what other types of assistance and support they need.

REFERRING LEADS

Since leads are the heart of any direct sales effort, you've got to be sure your people are developing good leads, either on their own or with your support.

Your own efforts can be extremely important for several reasons. Some new sales people will not know much about developing leads or prospecting, so they will look to you for guidance.

In some cases, new people will make their decisions about whether to sell your product or service based on whether you supply the leads. If you do, they can take it from there and make the sale. If you don't, they may feel lost and not know where to go or what to do. Providing leads and coordination assistance also helps avoid, or at least reduce, the problem of duplicate contacts.

Individual Leads

The first step in setting up a leads referral system is to research the target market yourself and obtain lists of individuals or organizations within this market.

Obvious sources of information are relevant groups you belong to or attended as a guest, or groups you know from close associates who are members. If you are a member, you may already have a membership directory or be able to get a membership list just by asking. Other groups provide lists to non-members or sell their membership lists.

As an example, suppose you have a product or service that appeals to professional career women in corporate management or running their own businesses. You could gather the membership rosters of the business women's groups throughout your area, such as the local chapter of the National Association for Professional Saleswomen.

You might also get membership lists from business groups with a large membership of professional women, such as members of a business breakfast group, the membership list of the Sales and Marketing Executives group, the roster of your local chapter of the National Speakers' Association, and so forth.

Still another source might be members of a singles or social group catering to a business and professional membership.

You should also watch current newspapers, magazines, and other media for possible leads. When you run across a useful idea, clip it out or write it down. For example, when I was working with a health program, I watched for ads selling other health products. Maybe these people would be interested in selling my health program. When I was involved in marketing travel, I regularly checked the travel section listings of groups that were sponsoring trips. Maybe some of them might be interested in taking one of our trips.

Group Leads

Besides lists of individuals, you might collect the names of groups, organizations, and companies. One good source for this might be the membership list of your local chamber of commerce. Some chambers provide lists of local associations and organizations as well.

There are also special business directories that may be useful, and here your library may help. For example, your local better business bureau might have a directory for its members. AT&T has a *Business Buyers Guide* in some cities.

There are all sorts of specialized yellow-page directories that may be helpful. For instance, you'll find directories for senior citizens (the Silver Pages), for ethnic groups (such as the Asian-American Directory), and for minority groups (such as the Gay Business Directory in San Francisco).

Still another possibility is an organization of organization leaders, such as the National Association for Association Executives and the Young President's Club.

Magazines and newspapers can also be a source of lists of companies. For example, some business publications, such as *Venture Magazine*, *California Business*, and your newspaper business section, may occasionally run lists of fast-growing companies or companies over a certain size, along with the name of company officers and an address.

Then, too, there are guides published by commercial publishers, some of which will be in your own library, such as *Contacts Influential*, which lists the names of high income individuals, and the *Corporate Meeting Planners Directory*, which lists the names of people who plan company programs.

Sources of Existing Lists

You can obtain lists of both individuals and companies from list brokers, and you can specify in detail exactly what type of person or organization you want to contact. You'll find these brokers listed in your local phone book under "mailing lists." Also, there are specialty list brokers, who specialize in lists of certain types, such as New Age Mailing, which offers lists of new age and spiritual groups.

Still other sources of lists are trade shows and conferences, which print programs listing exhibitors. If any of the exhibitors fall into your target market, then get a copy.

There are all sorts of sources for lists of individuals and organizations. Your task is to determine what kind would be most useful and research them by contacting your local library, business associations, associates, or list brokers.

Keeping List Files

As you gather list materials, organize them into files which you and your sales people can use for easy reference. For example, I used a Crate-A-File box for creating my own file, and then made up a manila folder for each category of leads. These included lists of speakers, women's groups and businesses, writers and media people, singles groups, nature and environmental groups, communications and media groups, health professionals and therapists, personal development and social groups, and miscellaneous leads. All were organized by city or area in the territory my sales team covered.

Choose the categories that make sense for your particular product or service, based on both the types of markets you expect to hit and the different geographic areas covered by your sales people. There may be some overlap from list to list, when people or groups are in several directories.

Distributing Leads

After you set up the categories and folders, let people in your group know about them. Encourage them to use the lists and let you know which ones they find useful.

If you have already established guidelines for dividing up sales areas, it may be obvious who can use each category. For example, someone covering women's groups would get any group in that category.

Alternatively, ask people to indicate which leads they are taking by starring those names and initialing them. If they use a list in full, they should note this fact by putting their names or initials on the list. Then, others will know not to make any contacts from that list.

If it's not possible to go through your lists and eliminate duplications, work out some way to handle the situation when the same prospect is called by two sales people. The usual policy is to let the person who makes the first contact handle that lead, unless there has been a long time lapse after the first contact or the initial contact has resulted in no sale.

In the latter case, the common policy is that the person who closes the sales gets the credit, unless it appears to be a joint contribution, in which case the commission is split.

Assigning Leads

Rather than leaving it up to your sales people to select their own leads for the leads file, you can make assignments yourself. This approach is especially good if you get call-ins or write-ins on an ad that needs to be handled right away, or if you pick up a current lead from a newspaper or magazine.

When you make assignments, use the geographic areas and categories worked out by your sales people as a guide. However, you should stay flexible in cases where there is a concentration of hot leads in a particular area. In this way you can immediately spread leads among your sales people so each one gets about the same number.

If you see your sales people at regular weekly meetings, you might simply put a copy of the leads in each person's file folder. For immediate action, especially if you feel it is an important lead, call the sales person and pass on the information.

Be sure to keep the original lists or copies of leads you give out. Make it clear that your sales people are welcome to make copies of any of the lists in the files they want to use, but they are not to take the lists out of the office.

Check up from time to time to make sure people are, in fact, contacting the leads they have taken. If they aren't, make these leads available again or reassign them. If there are any conflicts over who gets certain names, speak with the people involved and work it out so that each person gets approximately the same number of names.

TELEPHONE SCRIPTS, LETTERS, AND PRESENTATIONS

Even seasoned sales people may not know exactly how to present your product or service, so it helps to give them as much guidance as possible. One way is by suggesting telephone scripts, letters, and sales presentation guidelines.

Using Your Own Experience

The best way to develop such materials is through your own experience, based on what has worked for you. If you have done your own selling, you already have them on hand. Simply make copies and hand them out. Make it clear that these are materials you have used successfully, but that your sales people are welcome to adapt them as they wish to suit their own styles.

If you have sold your own product or service but haven't prepared any materials, then work on turning your experience into written form. One way to do this is to tape some of your phone calls or presentations. Have these typed up, then edit them to show the main sequence of points made in your call or presentation. You can hand this out as a sample script or presentation guideline.

You might want to combine sample scripts, letters, and guidelines into a small booklet or manual to pass out to your people. Take time at your orientations and training meetings to go over these materials.

Starting from Scratch

If you are introducing a new product or service or lack experience in selling, you can handle the development of scripts, letters, and presentation guidelines in two ways. One is to field test the approach yourself. Then, depending on your style, draft the guidelines you want to use, try them, and make modifications in response to prospective customers.

If you don't like to write and prefer to improvise, simply tape your calls and presentations until you have one you like. Then transcribe the tape and use that as a guide for your write-up.

Characteristics of Good Sales Materials

When you prepare sales materials, take into account your major types of customers, and if appropriate, develop separate telephone scripts, introductory or follow-up letters, and sales presentation guidelines for each category. Also, keep in mind the principles of good sales techniques described earlier.

Use a strong lead in your sample script, letter, or presentation to attract attention, quickly listing the major benefits to maintain interest. Likewise, try to trigger the prospect's desire for your product or service, be persuasive with your tone of assurance and conviction, and quickly move on to a close. In preparing materials, observe the following:

Be brief. Keep phone calls to about a minute.

A letter should consist of only a few paragraphs on a single page.

Get quickly to the point in stating your purpose.

Suggest a benefit targeted to the particular individual or organization being contacted.

Give information to establish the company's credentials.

Ask for action in the close, and set the stage for the next step in the sales process.

Provide materials for each step: initial call to find out whom to contact, introductory call, follow-up call, introductory letter, presentation.

AUDIO OR VIDEO PRESENTATIONS

Trips by you to the field are useful from time to time. However, on a long-term basis, your sales people will probably prefer to work alone. You can use audio and video tapes to provide them with sales ideas and a basis for discussing how to improve sales techniques.

If you record a live sales call, explain to the prospect why you are taping the call or presentation; legally, you're not supposed to record a conversation without informing the other person. Prospective customers are likely to be receptive. If not, they will say so.

Get permission in advance to videotape. Explain why you want to tape and make sure the person is completely supportive, since setting up lighting and sound can be disruptive to your sales presentation.

In either case, you can play it safe by recording a simulated sales call. Get a friend, associate, or someone on your sales team to play the role of the customer, while you make the call.

Procedure

Making audio tapes is fairly easy. If you're taping a telephone sales call, use a phone jack or a small pick-up microphone to connect the recorder to the telephone. If you're making a personal presentation, you can carry your tape recorder with you.

If you want to make a video tape, you will need to take one or possibly two additional people along. Only one person is needed if you're using an 8mm or VHS camcorder. Even an associate who knows how to use a video can do this. However, for more professional quality, go to 3/4-inch tape, and work with someone who is experienced in using this kind of camera. Also bring along someone to handle sound.

Presentation

Once you have made these audio or video tapes, invite your sales people to listen or view them at their own convenience. Or perhaps use them as part of your ongoing training program. In this case, allow l5 to 30 minutes for the presentation and additional time for discussion.

Call attention to the highlights of the presentation, such as the opening, presentation of benefits, techniques used to adapt the presentation to the interest and needs of the particular customer, and the steps used to close. Also, allow time for comments and feedback, and answer any questions that come up.

LIVE PRESENTATIONS OR DEMONSTRATIONS

As your sales group grows, you can provide support and stimulate sales by putting on live presentations or demonstrations for sales people and their prospective customers. You'll also find such presentations a good selling point when prospective sales people are deciding whether or not to join your company.

Planning the Presentation

It will help in preparing your presentation if you can first attend those put on by others. Notice what information they cover, how they present it, and what techniques seem to work especially well. Also, notice what questions come up frequently so that you can be prepared to answer them. Through planning, you can determine what to include and how to organize it so the presentation goes well. In doing your planning, keep these points in mind.

Be brief. A good presentation is short and to the point. Present the essential facts about your product or service in an interesting way and answer any questions that come up. The key to an effective presentation is to entertain and involve your audience as well as inform.

Stress benefits. As in sales generally, the stress should be on benefits, why the prospective customer should want your product or service. The program should build to a close, so that your sales people can then take over with the necessary applications or order forms. Since the average person remembers only about 10 to 20% of what is heard, you should emphasize and repeat key points.

Use illustrations and demonstrations where you can, since people remember about 30% of what they see. Also, visual materials have immediate impact. To make your presentation entertaining, include a few anecdotes or personal experiences, highlighting key points and adding color.

Be prepared. If presentations are new to you, don't worry about being nervous. As you get used to speaking and making group presentations, your nervousness will subside. In fact, many talented, well-paid speakers have a twinge of nervousness before they go in front of an audience. They actually tend to perform better as a result, because they put that nervous energy into their performance.

The best way to reduce anxiety is knowing exactly what you want to say. Then you'll be more confident when you start. Once you begin, focus on your audience and concentrate on your material, not on yourself. Soon you'll be totally involved in your presentation and won't have a chance to feel nervous.

Organizing the Presentation

Organize your presentation or demonstration to last about 45 minutes to an hour, allowing about 15 minutes for people to arrive. Plan on about 15 minutes at the end of the presentation for your sales people to wind up the session.

Opener. The key is to start with a good opener to attract attention, such as a product demonstration, presentation of startling statistics to show why your program is needed, or present slides of people using your product. Then structure the program so that it is well-organized and compact.

Ask your audience to save questions for the end. Allow about 10 minutes for questions, but not much longer, because people may bring up all sorts of trivia. It's better to invite those who still have unanswered questions to wait until the formal meeting breaks up. Afterward, you'll be amazed at how many of those seemingly burning questions disappear.

Expect to include most of the same basic information you would in a good one-on-one presentation. But add a little bit more "sizzle," so your presentation has added impact. There are many possible ways to do this. For example, start with or include a slide-sound presentation or film about how your product or service works. Use a flip chart with pictures, graphs, or other visuals.

Use others. If you have several people who can do different parts of the presentation, so much the better. That adds strength and substance to what you are saying.

If you have someone who is an especially good motivator, have that person lead off to get everyone's attention and increase the excitement and interest level. Later, that person can close the demonstration to better motivate everyone to act right away.

Handling handouts. As in a one-on-one presentation, provide informative handouts or brochures about your company and its products or services which people can take home. Depending on your meeting format, you might have these available as people arrive so they can read them while they are waiting.

If a sales person brings an entire group, it may be better to distribute materials after the meeting, or let the sales person hand them out. In this way the sales person stays more in control.

Presentation categories. In organizing your presentation, use the same basic categories as you would in putting on an effective one-on-one presentation, selecting those categories which are appropriate to your program. These include the following:

Introduction.
Information on the product or service.
Background information on your company.
Description of any backup support your company provides in using the product or service.
A brief question-and-answer period.
A close in which you ask for some action such as an order, and turn over the follow-up to your sales people.

Working Out the Logistics

To make sure your meeting flows smoothly and professionally, work out the logistics in advance. Even if it's a meeting with only a handful of people, plan it well. Give your sales people plenty of advance notice and make the event seem special.

For example, besides the small presentations you hold on a regular basis, you might hold a special meeting once a month, building it up as a special rally or presentation. Perhaps even invite a special motivational speaker.

Encourage your sales people to make calls and invite guests. Keep in touch with them to keep them motivated. If they are having trouble, suggest how they can do it.

Dress well. Dress to make a good impression. The usual rule here is to dress a little more formally than you might at a small informal presentation. This helps to give you a success image, which contributes to making sales.

Generally, men should wear a conservative suit or sports jacket and slacks. Women should wear a dress, business suit, or fashionable pantsuit. The idea is to dress for success, because that image carries over to your product or service.

Set up early. Get everything properly set up in advance. Plan to arrive early with everything you need before the meeting, and give yourself plenty of time to set up. Then, check everything. If you're going to give a food demonstration, be sure the stove or hot plate works and know how long it's going to take you to prepare the food. Likewise, if you're showing slides or a video, check the projector and the video-screen connection.

Keep the tone friendly and informal. If this is a small meeting at your home or office, keep in mind the following points. Have coffee or light refreshments on hand and invite people to help themselves before the presentation. This allows people to mix and mingle before the meeting starts. Place chairs in a circle or semicircle so people won't feel they are in a classroom or theater.

Start on time. If guests are late or don't show up, start the meeting anyway, no later than 15 minutes after it was scheduled to begin. Often some of the invited guests won't show up. Don't worry about it or express concern to others. It's not fair to delay the meeting for latecomers. If they arrive late, invite them to join the meeting quietly, answering questions about what they missed later. Don't try to start the meeting over, a sure way to antagonize the people who were on time.

Introductions. Start with appropriate introductions to make everyone feel comfortable. In some cases, it may make sense to start with brief introductions. Often, people are interested in knowing a little about other people in the group and why they are there. In other cases, names are enough.

In a small meeting setting introductions are appropriate since everyone is sitting in a small area, commonly in a semicircle or circle. If everyone knows everyone else, of course, dispense with this. Say a little about yourself and how you happened to get involved with this company, product, or service. Perhaps introduce other sales people with your company. Then go into the presentation, using the format you've already prepared.

Setting up Larger Meetings

If you are organizing a larger meeting, you'll need to do a bit more groundwork to coordinate arrangements. Also, you should work to build advance excitement to encourage a good showing. There are several things to do in preparing for the meeting.

Choice of location. Once meeting attendance grows beyond the number you can accommodate in your home or office, you will need to find a larger site. Besides considering size, consider how the meeting location contributes to your professional image.

Choose a site in keeping with the image of your product or service, and your selected target market. For instance, if you're selling a high-cost product to a business and professional market, use a nice hotel or restaurant for your meeting. If your product is for a lower income, blue-collar market, perhaps use a church, bank meeting room, or your local YMCA.

Other possible sites include large apartment complexes with conference rooms, lodges and other public buildings. Also, choose a site that is centrally located to your market and easy to get to by public transportation as well as by car. The key here is suitability.

If you know someone who puts on a lot of parties or other events, ask for recommended locations. And if you happen to visit a place that looks suitable, ask the manager about using it.

Room size. Estimate how large a space you will need based on the number of people your sales people think they can recruit and how your publicity is likely to pull.

Ask people to RSVP so you can plan accordingly. If the response is great, organize a second meeting and obtain a larger room. Alternatively, if the response is low, move to a smaller room at the same location.

Find out in advance how many people are coming. Ask your sales people to estimate how many guests they are bringing, so you can prepare sufficient literature, refreshments, product samples, chairs, and the like. Not all of your sales people will let you know, and inevitably some people who say they will come, won't, while others will show up unannounced. But at least you will have a rough idea of how many to expect.

Room arrangements. Work out room arrangements in advance. When you use a commercial meeting space, the standard theater or classroom arrangement with a podium, blackboard, flip charts, and/or audiovisual equipment usually works best. It looks professional and focuses attention on the speaker.

Check in advance to see what equipment is supplied, and arrange to supply the rest yourself. Find out, too, if the management will arrange the room the way you want it before the meeting, and if so, give the manager the necessary instructions. If not, allow extra time to do this before the meeting. And if you need to return the room to its original arrangement after the meeting, allow time for that, too.

Advance preparation. Big sales presentations are no time to improvise, though you do want to leave room for spontaneity. When several people are contributing, decide in advance what they are to say. If your sales people are fairly new at giving presentations, rehearse a few times. Make sure all participants know their parts, and work out smooth transitions from one person to another. Also work out a rough timetable for each part of the presentation, and remind everyone to stick to it.

Determine which product samples, handouts, and audiovisual or other equipment are necessary. In this way, you won't discover that something is missing in the middle of your presentation. Also, decide who should be responsible for preparing materials, and allow plenty of time to prepare them. The checklist on the next page will help you.

SALES PRESENTATION BOOK

Another support tool is the presentation book. If you are already using your own book for presentations, you can show it to your people. Emphasize that they can follow your example or modify it to suit their own styles. Explain that a presentation book is an excellent tool for impressing prospective customers, since it pulls together information about your product or service in a systematic, attractive way.

Point out that the presentation book should be designed to highlight benefits and arranged to follow the presentation format to avoid flipping back and forth, which can look unprofessional. For flexibility and to make different presentations to different customers, the presentation book should be in a loose leaf binder that allows the order to be easily changed. Clear plastic sleeves which slip into a notebook are ideal, since their contents can easily be changed.

Group Presentation Checklist

Date of Meeting:
Speakers/Participants:
Location:

Materials Needed	Items Needed	Who Is Getting Needed Items
Equipment:		
Literature:		
Refreshments:		
Other:		

Topic	Speakers	Item Needed	Person Responsible
1.			
2.			
3.			

Contents

Suggest to your sales people that they include the various promotional materials you have developed, such as flyers, brochures, questions and answers about your product or service, and testimonial letters. In addition, they should include materials they have developed, such as letters of appreciation and support from customers, price comparisons with competing products, and informational brochures on the field.

Sample Sequence

You might also provide a list of suggested items to include and a suggested order. For example, a book to accompany a presentation might be arranged like this:

Flyers highlighting the products or services you offer.
Detailed brochures describing each product or service in depth.
Customized features you offer to adapt your product or service to
the customer.

Special meetings or demonstrations you offer to explain your
product or service in more detail.
Background information on your company and on the development of
your product or service.
Articles that have appeared about your product or service or about
your field generally.
Ads you have run in national or local publications.
A list of questions and answers about your product or service.
Sample price comparisons with the competition.
Testimonial letters from customers.
Examples of awards or recognition received.
Photographs of people using your product or service.
Price breakdowns, discount rates, purchase policies and procedures.
Application forms, order forms, and registration forms.

Note that in a presentation book, as in your presentation, the
information on price and ordering the product or service comes last,
after you have established the value of what you are selling. Pricing
and ordering or sign-up information becomes relevant when you are
about ready to close.

Uses

Besides talking about content and order, you might suggest ways to use a
presentation book, too. When I sit down with a customer I flip through
the book as I bring up different topics, showing examples to illustrate
my point. I use my presentation book to reinforce my statements.

In some cases, it is helpful to give people who are just getting
started a presentation book which is already organized. They may not
be sure what to do or say, so an organized book helps them as they flip
through the pages covering the topics illustrated. However, people
should create their own books as soon as possible. In this way their
books are organized to match their presentations in their own styles.

GETTING REGULAR FEEDBACK

Regular feedback is necessary to find out what kind of support or
assistance your people need. At regular sales meetings, ask people
what kind of support they would like from you. Also invite them to
contact you personally if they prefer, and emphasize that you are
always ready to listen.

Tell them you want to provide whatever support or assistance they need, and you need their input. In some cases, people may resist telling you anything that is critical or negative. They will hold back at meetings and won't see you alone. But once the group is large enough to provide anonymity, you can use a questionnaire to find out what people need or would like changed.

Using Questionnaires

When using a questionnaire, explain that you are using it to get information about what people need, and assure everyone that they can fill them out anonymously. In this way, people can feel free to say whatever they want, even if it is critical. Encourage them to be open and honest; you want to hear exactly what they think, both the good and the bad.

Keep the questionnaires short: one page or at most two. You can use multiple-choice questions for getting a general response, such as how people feel about your support generally. But if you want specific comments, use open-ended questions and ask people to be specific. (See the sample questionnaire on the next page.)

Evaluating the Questionnaires

When you review the questionnaires, it's easier to get an overview of what everyone thinks by looking at all the answers to the same question together. On the open-ended questions, read all of the answers to one question first. You may find a general flavor and that may give you enough information without a more formal analysis.

If there seem to be specific points raised, note each theme or category and make a tally mark each time it occurs. Those with the most marks tell you which issues are most important to your sales people. With multiple-choice questions, also keep a tally. The totals for each category will give you a picture of the overall response.

By doing this for every question, you will have an overall picture of what your people would like from you. Then, you can act accordingly.

It's a good idea to report back to the group on the results of your survey, so that they will know you are responding directly to their concerns. If you plan to respond to a request, indicate this and explain what you are going to do and when. If a point has come up several times but you can't do anything about it, mention this and explain why you can't deal with it at this time.

Questionnaire on Group Needs

This questionnaire is designed to find out what kind of assistance and support you would like from me and how you feel about what I am already doing. Please answer as openly and honestly as you can. Don't sign your name, since the questionnaire is designed to be anonymous. I will institute as many of your suggested changes as I can.

1. How do you feel generally about the kind of support and assistance I am providing? (Please check one.)

____Excellent   ____Good   ____Average   ____Fair   ____Poor

2. Why do you feel the way you do?

3. What types of assistance and support do you consider the most helpful to you? (Please be specific.)

4. What do you like, if anything, about the type of assistance and support you are getting? What would you like to see changed? (Please be specific.)

5. What other kinds of assistance and support would you like to see added? What other ways can I help with your sales?

17
Training Sales People
to Train Others

After your sales team is established and successfully selling your product or service, the next step in expanding your sales capability is training your sales people to train others. By multiplying the number of sales trainers, you create tremendous possibilities for company growth.

A key consideration here, of course, is that your product or service must lend itself to this kind of growth. If you are selling something which has a specialized market, or which involves limited production, it may make more sense to maintain a small specialized sales force to keep up with either demand or production. But if you've got something with broad appeal which you can provide in large quantities, you can think big about sales.

WHEN TO BEGIN

A timetable for training sales leaders can be incorporated into your original business plan. Or you can wait until your sales group has grown to a certain size before delegating leadership or training to others. Either approach works fine.

The important point is to start delegating training and creating new managers once your sales team has more than five to ten people. Beyond this size, you usually can't supervise and motivate your people effectively, and you lose the personal touch necessary to good sales management.

APPROACHES AND SOURCES

One approach is to hire new people specifically to become sales managers. Another is to promote from within. Or you can use one of the established, more complex methods of creating a marketing network through franchising or organizing a multi-level marketing organization.

Franchising and MLM are complex undertakings requiring specified legal procedures, which I will not go into here. However, some of the successful principles used in these approaches can be incorporated in your own program, namely training others to sell as successfully as you do, and showing them how to pass on these skills by teaching others to sell.

Hiring Managers Before Hiring Sales People

If you hire people to manage before you create your sales group, you can turn over to them much or all of the recruiting. You provide the product or service plus sales and training materials. But it's up to them to advertise or contact potential sales people. Alternatively, you can assist by running an ad for sales people yourself, and turning over the replies to your sales leaders for follow-up.

A good example of this approach is a company that sells clothes imported from Italy. They advertised for sales managers, interviewed the applicants, and selected seven. The company provided them with a list of policies and commission arrangements, catalogs, order forms, and other sales materials. The company also held several training meetings and made their offices available to the new managers for making calls, typing letters, and holding meetings.

The managers were then instructed to advertise for their own sales people. The company continued to do its own advertising, referring calls to the new managers. The results were spectacular. Within months the company had a strong team of four managers from the seven it had initially hired. Each had about a half dozen sales people selling clothes through a party plan presentation.

At the beginning, the company had no sales people and just a few clothing samples, catalog sheets, and order forms. By skillfully creating an effective sales organization with a few key managers, the company in just a few months was grossing nearly $10,000 a month.

Hiring Managers From Outside the Group

In hiring new people to train and manage sales people, you can use the same criteria discussed earlier for selecting one sales manager. Select people who are good in working with people, take the initiative, act in a positive manner, have a sales background, and have a good track record in training or managing others.

Since you are hiring several managers to split up training and sales responsibilities, it is important to make clear the division of responsibility, in order to avoid conflict. A good way to do this is to divide up your sales area into territories or to split up the markets you cover, such as corporations, retail stores, wholesalers, individuals, groups, churches, educational institutions, and so on.

Easing in new managers. It's tricky bringing in outsiders. It often works well to introduce the new people at a regular sales meeting and give them a chance to describe their backgrounds. You might even do this before you decide which applicants to hire, using the reactions of your sales people as a guide in making your decisions.

Invite your sales people to introduce themselves, and provide some time for mingling after the meeting. In deciding who would work best together, notice which newcomers and current employees mix well, and use information you have about their interests and backgrounds.

Creating new slots for managers. Another possibility is to continue to work with some or all of your present sales people, while bringing in mangers to develop their own new sales groups in other areas. In this case, the transition will typically be smoother, since your current sales people won't have to make the transition from you to a new manager.

You should reassure your current people by explaining exactly what you are doing and how these new people will be incorporated into the organization. Moreover, you should be careful to assign these managers who are going to develop their own sales teams to territories or markets that are not already covered.

Promoting from Your Own Sales Group

The alternative to hiring outside sales managers is to select people from your sales group who have leadership potential and promote them. Promotions from within improve morale, and training is likely to be smoother and quicker than with someone unfamiliar with your organization.

If you do want to promote from within, notice which of your sales people show leadership abilities, and train them to train and manage others. You may want to set up criteria for promotion into sales management, such as achieving a certain monthly sales volume.

Gaining group acceptance. One of the main sources of conflict in any organization is resentment when one person is promoted over another. The person who is not promoted may be disappointed and feel a lower sense of self-esteem. There may be envy or resentment in spite of admiration for the person doing well.

To reduce negative feelings, it's a good idea to recognize the person being promoted and to emphasize the reasons for the promotion, showing that the promotion is appropriate and fair. For example, at a regular sales meeting, you might announce a promotion and then go over the person's achievements. Or you might do this in a separate recognition ceremony.

Explaining the promotion. It is also important to explain what the promotion means to the group as a whole, so people feel reassured about their own positions in the organization. A frequent concern of sales people is that someone will move in on their territories, so you need to clarify the situation if there are going to be any changes in territories.

It's also important to put the promotion in a positive light for the organization itself. One way to do this is by pointing out how these new people can benefit the group. For instance, you might mention that there will be extra training and coordination, and operations will run more smoothly. The new people will be exploring new markets and developing leads, which will be turned over to the current sales people.

You can turn promotions into an advantage by showing how they will help each sales person, as well as the people being promoted. This will facilitate acceptance by your sales group, and make it easier for people newly promoted to perform their new jobs.

WORKING WITH NEW SALES LEADERS

Once you have selected your new sales leaders and worked out procedures for easing them into your organization, the final step is training. They must be trained to work with your sales people and, perhaps, even train new people to work with their own sales groups. (This is the principle that makes some multi-level companies so successful.)

In training these new leaders, you should show how to do what you have been doing. If they have had previous experience in sales management, your main task will be to help them adapt their skills to your particular sales approach. If they lack management experience, you will need to help them develop management skills. In either case, there are several strategies for training your new sales leaders.

Meetings

Hold regular sales management meetings in addition to sales meetings. Sales management meetings should be designed to plan overall strategies for the organization, so your sales leaders can pass this information on to their sales people. This is also an opportunity to get feedback from your sales leaders about what is happening in the field to aid you in deciding what to produce and how to best sell it.

Use these meetings to determine what kind of training your sales people and managers need. Determine what sales materials and product literature they need, and ask for suggestions about content and method of presentation. These meetings can also be used to plan joint sales activities, such as participating in trade shows and setting up large-scale demonstrations and events.

Observation

Invite your sales leaders to join you at product or service demonstrations, sales presentations, and at your regular sales meetings, so they can observe and use you as a model. Naturally, sales leaders should develop their own leadership styles, but they can get ideas on how to do it from watching you.

They can start off by observing, with time afterward for discussion and feedback. Then, gradually, they might participate in various parts of the program, until they feel free to do it all themselves.

Participation

Ask your sales leaders to set up meetings and training activities for their own sales people. You can provide overall meetings, presentations, training sessions, rallies, conventions, and the like. However, your sales leaders should hold similar smaller scale events on their own.

They should report to you on their activities and get your suggestions at the sales management meetings. Otherwise, they should be free to use their own ideas in managing their own groups. Encourage your people to take the initiative and they will feel more involved and committed.

Training

Provide your sales leaders with regular training on sales management. These meetings should be designed to help your sales leaders in recruiting and working with members of their own sales groups. You might consider setting up an ongoing training program that follows the basic steps described earlier. In fact, you might provide each person with a copy of this book to use in training. In addition, allow plenty of time for feedback and discussion of any problems your managers are having with their groups so you can help resolve them.

Tone. In working with your sales leaders, think of your organization as a pyramid with a chain of command going from you to your sales leaders and then to the sales people under them. You provide general guidance and set the tone for the type of organization you want. You convey that through your meetings and training, so your leaders can pass it on to their own sales people.

Feedback. You must remain open and responsive to feedback from all of your sales people. For efficiency, set up channels of communication for sales people to communicate to their leaders, who communicate to you. But also be flexible. If there are communication breakdowns, you should be able to communicate directly with sales people in any sales group and they should be able to communicate directly with you.

Normally, people shouldn't expect to do this. Encourage them to use the usual channels, so your sales leaders can maintain their central role of leading their sales people. Yet, if problems develop, you will want to hear about them. That's why people should know that they can come directly to you.

CONCLUSION

This book focuses on the process of building an effective sales organization which you manage yourself. Once you get to the point where you have a team of sales leaders, you are ready to expand into a national organization with a solid, growing sales force.

Are you ready to go on? Do you have a product or service mix to do it? Can you count on enough supply to meet the growing demand as your sales force grows? There are all sorts of issues to consider as you think about expanding. With an effective sales organization you can do it.

Index

978-0-595-46486-9
0-595-46486-6